New Studies in the Philosophy of Religion

General Editor: W. D. Hudson, Reader in Moral Philosophy,
University of Exeter

This series of monographs includes studies of all the main
problems in the philosophy of religion. It will be of particular
interest to those who study this subject in universities or colleges.
The philosophical problems connected with religious belief are
not, however, a subject of concern only to specialists; they arise
in one form or another for all intelligent men when confronted
by the appeals or the claims of religion.

The general approach of this series is from the standpoint of
contemporary analytical philosophy, and the monographs are
written by a distinguished team of philosophers, all of whom
now teach, or have recently taught, in British or American
universities. Each author has been commissioned to analyse
some aspect of religious belief; to set forth clearly and concisely
the philosophical problems which arise from it; to take into
account the solutions which classical or contemporary philosophers have offered; and to present his own critical assessment
of how religious belief now stands in the light of these problems
and their proposed solutions.

In the main it is theism with which these monographs deal,
because that is the type of religious belief with which readers
are most likely to be familiar, but other forms of religion are not
ignored. Some of the authors are religious believers and some
are not, but it is not their primary aim to write polemically,
much less dogmatically, for or against religion. Rather, they
set themselves to clarify the nature of religious belief in the light
of modern philosophy by bringing into focus the questions about
it which a reasonable man as such has to ask. How is talk of
God like, and how unlike, other universes of discourse in which
men engage, such as science, art or morality? Is this talk of
God self-consistent? Does it accord with other rational beliefs
which we hold about man or the world which he inhabits? It
is questions such as these which this series will help the reader
to answer for himself.

New Studies in the Philosophy of Religion

IN THE SAME SERIES

Published

In preparation

The Concept of Worship

NINIAN SMART
Professor of Religious Studies, University of Lancaster

Macmillan
St. Martin's Press

First published 1972 by
THE MACMILLAN PRESS LTD
London and Basingstoke
Associated companies in New York Toronto
Dublin Melbourne Johannesburg and Madras

Library of Congress catalog card no. 72–77773

SBN 333 10273 8

Printed in Great Britain by
R & R CLARK LTD
Edinburgh

Contents

General Editor's Preface

Professor Ninian Smart has attempted in this monograph to analyse a concept which, if any, is central to religious belief and experience. He begins by asking what can – within the normal use of the word 'worship' – be worshipped. This leads him to discuss such matters as the use of ritual, the relatively public nature of concepts of the Focus of worship, the indispensable necessity of intention in worship, the issues raised when the object of worship is believed to be omnipresent, the need to see God as a concept formed in the milieu of worship, and so on. After saying what it is for God to be an object of worship, Professor Smart turns his attention to what may follow from this so far as philosophical questions concerning the existence of God are concerned – e.g. to the view that in order to be a worthy object of worship God must be a necessary, not a contingent, being and the consequent problems which have arisen within the philosophy of religion concerning God's necessary existence.

The author of this study has an equipment to conduct it which is exceedingly rare. He has an encyclopaedic knowledge of comparative religion and is a trained analytical philosopher. The points which he makes are clear and precise and the material used to illustrate them is handled with expert ease. The product is an erudite, readable and penetrating study which will not only be valuable to the student of philosophy of religion but of interest to all readers who find religion a fascinating and important matter.

W. D. HUDSON

University of Exeter

Preface

The aim of this monograph is to explore the concept of worship. In some degree the method is linguistic, but it is aimed also to place the activity of worship in the milieu of religious practices and beliefs. The philosophy of religion must always remember the variety of religious traditions. However, for the sake of familiarity of examples, I shall pay more attention to the Christian tradition than to others.

NINIAN SMART

PART ONE

Worshipping

1.1. *The problem of the range of entities.* One central issue about the idea of worship concerns the range of entities that can be worshipped. That is, what range of entities can be objects of worship? This is different, of course, from the question of what objects one should worship. Maybe there should be only one such entity, the true God. But that value-judgement differs from the issue of what entities it makes sense to worship. Or to put it more linguistically, can we delimit the range of objects properly taken by the verb 'to worship'?

1.2. *God or gods?* One hypothesis is that typically what is worshipped is a god or God. The hypothesis of course raises the question of criteria – what counts as a god or God? It would not of course do to suppose that a god is a being who is worshipped (though this is tempting), for then the hypothesis collapses into an analytic truth. In any case the hypothesis might be countered by such examples as the following: 'Henry worships his stomach' and 'Karl worships money'. It is strained to count Henry's stomach as a god, however metaphorically apt it may be.

1.3. *Dealing with the metaphor.* We feel that in the counter-examples 'worship' is being used analogically or metaphorically, and not in a literal way. This is a tricky position to establish. For one thing there is notoriously a difficulty about producing criteria for the contrast between the literal and the non-literal. Sometimes a word, at some point in its history, may be used literally in a sense A and metaphorically in sense B; but then at another point in its history the sense B becomes the literal usage. For instance, the verb 'to broadcast' in olden days referred to a method of sowing seed, and metaphorically was used in connection with radio and television. Nowadays, however, the latter sense would usually be taken to be its literal usage.

1.4. *The metaphor and superimposition.* A second problem arises from the fact that the concept of worship is often applied in what

3

I have elsewhere called a 'superimposed' manner. That is, the concept is superimposed on others. For instance, an activity which can be described without implying any overt religious meaning can be counted as falling under a religious one – where worship is, so to say, extended from Sunday to the rest of the week. The point is put in the well-known hymn:

> A servant with this clause
> Makes drudgery divine;
> Who sweeps a room as for Thy laws
> Makes that and the action fine.

Also consider: 'The sacrifices of God are a broken spirit.' A weaker kind of superimposition can be said to occur where a non-religious activity or entity becomes a rival to a religious one – like worshipping Mammon rather than God. All this makes it less easy to say that 'He worships his stomach' is *merely* a metaphor.

1.5. *Replying to the metaphor problem.* Although it is very hard or impossible to invent a tidy doctrine of metaphor and of analogy, we can deal with the above problems by appeal to convention (and if a different convention were canvassed, that would not matter either – we should simply appeal to that: the point is to make adequate distinctions). The present usage of 'worship' is such that a certain range of questions about worship is quite natural. About a group of people, we can ask whom they worship, whether they use incense in their worship, whether they use music and if so of what kind. These questions become laughable in relation to the stomach. Furthermore, on the assumption that the statement 'Henry worships his stomach' is not being used in a religious or pious way – for instance, it is not being used in the context of a homily or by someone with special religious commitments – one can give an adequate alternative account of what is being said. On this assumption, what the statement amounts to is that Henry places a very high value on eating and that consequently a number of other activities are subordinated to eating. The alternative rendering does not incorporate any notion of worship as such. By contrast it would be a hard task to give an alternative account of a description of religious worship. To say that someone worships God is not adequately rendered by saying that he places a very

4

high value upon God, even though he would be inconsistent to worship God and not place a high value on him.

1.6. *Superimposition and intentions.* These last remarks are also very relevant to the matter of superimposition. For even though sweeping a room may count as a form of worship, this is only seriously so when the person sweeping the room *intends* his action not merely as sweeping but also as worshipping. For him to intend this, he has to employ the concept of worshipping and more particularly of worshipping, say, *God* – and these concepts he basically learns elsewhere. One does not learn the primary concept of worship (in the conventional usage) by sweeping floors but by participating in and/or observing acts of worship such as singing hymns, addressing prayers to God and so on. Thus one can make a distinction between a merely metaphorical use of 'to worship', and the serious analogical use which depends upon acceptance of the primary duty of worship. We may note then that in the analogical use, as in the primary use, the idea of worship has to do with intentions.

1.7. *The use of ritual.* However, at the same time the core idea of worship has to do with ritual. To worship is to perform a piece of ritual. This is the sort of thing that can be repeated at intervals, can last a certain time, can be done quickly or slowly. The question of arriving at a proper account of worship can thus be approached from two directions – from the outer direction of ritual and from the 'inner' direction of intentions and beliefs. What, however, is a ritual? It is worth while starting with some very elementary observations. A ritual typically involves some kind of overt action. I say 'typically' here because it is possible to think of queer examples where the overt disappears. For instance, if praying (for, say, an Episcopalian) involves kneeling, a person can learn to pray and then pray by imagining himself kneeling. He does it all 'in his head'. But ritual typically has to do with overt, and chiefly bodily, action (physical instruments are of course used, but it is very rare to have the instruments working by themselves with no bodily action – a rare case is the Tibetan prayer-wheel).

1.8. *Variations and the 'bowing down' simplification.* The overt actions vary, of course, very widely from one ritual to another and from one culture to another. Some people pray standing, others kneeling, others sitting; some with eyes closed and others with eyes open. Thus worship takes on a wide variety of ritual

5

manifestations. However, in order to simplify the discussion, let us assume that it in fact involves a *standard* bodily action, namely bowing down. One can get more easily thus to the heart of the matter. Since worship, on this supposition, involves bowing down, we can ask what this physical movement symbolises. To this we shall return shortly; but in the meantime let us note that bowing down is more than a physical movement; or rather that the use of this bodily movement to express worship involves more than a physical movement.

1.9. *Body and mind in bowing down.* To bow down is to bend the body in a certain way. But obviously 'Henry bows down before the image of the god' does not mean the same as 'Henry bends his body in front of the image of the god'. For instance, Henry may be being shown round a temple by a guide who takes him through a low doorway in front of an image of a god. To get through the doorway he has to bend his body, and he bends his body in front of the god's image. But he would not be bowing down before the image of the god. Thus bowing down before the image might entail bending the body in front of the image, but the latter does not entail the former. What then is the 'overplus' in the notion of bowing down before the image of a god? First, bending the body is by implication connected with (indeed, directed at) the image and presumably with the god. (We later need to explore what the relationship is between image and god.) A merely spatial description of the scene would not suffice, and in particular we should notice that 'before' is not being used literally. Consider the following attempt to put the matter in merely spatial terms: 'The upper part of Henry's body inclines forward at an angle to the lower part, so that the upper part is on average six inches nearer the image than the lower part, which is ten feet from Henry on a straight line running perpendicularly from a line drawn through Henry's hips. . . .' In other words, the term 'before' has two facets to its meaning. On the one hand, the worshipper is literally (spatially) in front of the image. On the other hand the image is, so to say, the phenomenological focus of his activity. One can compare it with such a statement as 'Henry waved to Mary'. This involves bodily movement, the movement of an arm and hand, but it also involves the movement's being directed as a signal to the other person.

1.10. *Restrictions on bowing down.* Are there restrictions to be

6

placed upon the phenomenological foci? Could Henry, though he is bowing down in front of an image of the goddess Kali, claim that he is really doing homage to Christ given that there is as it happens an image of Christ right behind Henry's back? Normally this would strike us as an absurd claim, though with a bit of strain we can make up a sort of story to make some sense of it. For instance: 'Henry is bowing before the image of Kali, but Kali and Christ are really one, so that in worshipping Kali he is worshipping Christ, who also happens to be manifested in an image behind Henry's back.' Such a story might, I suppose, be supplied by a very ecumenically minded Hindu. There are of course problems about such a story – problems about the criteria of identity as between different gods (to which we shall in due course need to return). But leaving aside the story, the claim to be doing homage to Christ does not sound at all right. The reason is in a way an elementary one, namely that there is a conventional, symbolic element in a ritual; and in the case of bowing down the rule is that bowing down to cannot be per-formed with your back to the focus. It is rather like taking your hat off to someone who is standing immediately behind you, when there are no mirrors in front to make it feasible.

1.11. *Ritual and conventional meaning.* The usage of physical movements in ritual supplies a range of gestures, and these in a sense constitute a language. One can misuse gestures, as you can misuse words. If I describe birds following a ship as seagulls when they clearly are not seagulls, then this is good evidence that I do not grasp the meaning of 'seagull'. If having observed someone cock a snook at someone else I think that this is a nice friendly gesture, and cock a snook at the vicar next time I see him, then I have failed to grasp the meaning of a snook-cock. If therefore I imagine that bowing down in the direction of an image of Ganesh I am really saluting an image of Christ behind my back, I fail to understand the gesture-language of worship. So for the observer one way to pick out the object of worship is to look in the direction in which the worshipper is bowing. This may not always be an easy way, of course, since some people worship imageless, invisible gods. We shall have to return to this problem; but meanwhile let us continue with the supposition of the image. But of course when I pick out Ganesh as the god that is being worshipped by the fact that the image is a Ganesh one, there still remains the question of the sense, if any, in which

Ganesh is identified with the image. Let us put the matter in the following way. Suppose I wish to pick out what it is that is attracting the rapt attention of a friend of mine looking out of the window; and suppose I use the method of following his gaze. This may bring me to identify the focus of his interest as being a squirrel on the lawn. But the business is different in connection with Ganesh; for literally what is in front of the worshipper and being the focus of his attention (seemingly) is a block of cunningly carved stone. Yet it is not sensible to say that the person is worshipping a piece of stone. Or rather it is only sensible in making a particular sort of point, as follows.

1.12. *The extra-perspectival description.* In Bishop Heber's hymn 'From Greenland's icy mountains . . .' he describes the heathen as bowing down to wood and stone. Surely the meaning is that the heathen foolishly and wrongfully worship wood and stone. But it is not much use simply replying that that is not how the heathen look at it (relevant as this is from the point of view of the phenomenology of religion). Heber is trying to make a certain point, namely that though the heathen may conceive himself to be worshipping a spiritual entity or whatever it is that is 'in' or identified somehow with the image, he is just wrong, for there is but one God, and that is the invisible God who eschews images and who was revealed through the Old and New Testaments. That roughly is what Heber means. So there turns out to be a sense in which the heathen is actually worshipping a block of stone (vainly imagining other things). How can we understand this comment? One could describe it as a point made from another perspective. There are secular analogies. Thus it is not unknown for non-fans of football to describe a game as twenty-two grown men chasing a piece of leather round a field. This is a literally correct account, so far as it goes; but it fails to bring out the meaning of the activity for the people who participate in the game, and follow it. Thus the piece of leather in question is not just a piece of leather. It is the ball – it is something to get into the back of the opponents' net, according to the rules governing the notion of scoring a goal. There is nothing peculiar in handling a piece of leather as such; but in the context of football this is a foul (except for the goal-keepers of course), a taboo action, and if deliberately done, 'dirty'. So for the participants and the followers the piece of leather is, as it were, loaded with meanings, caveats, taboos.

8

Thus one needs to consider descriptions coming from differing perspectives. For the non-fan, there are twenty-two men chasing a piece of leather. For the fan there are two teams each of eleven men, playing elaborately, one representing one town or community or club and the other another. Likewise from the perspective of the worshipper the image is not just a piece of stone. Rather it is in some way the locus of the god. But from the Christian-missionary perspective, as represented by Heber, there is but one God and there is no Ganesh. So from that perspective the heathen is in fact worshipping a block of stone. From the point of view of phenomenology Bishop Heber gets low marks, but about that he would not be dismayed. He would, however, be in deep trouble in understanding the concept of worship if he could not grasp some phenomenological focus or other of worship, in his case the Christian God.

1.13. *Extra-perspectival description and critical judgement.* The typical point of the extra-perspectival description, where given deliberately, is to express a judgement, disdaining that which is described. Normally the description to the effect that twenty-two grown men are chasing a bit of leather round a field is meant to be deflationary and disdainful. Even stronger would be a case like this: 'Henry is in love with a gold-digging tart.' If Henry in fact is in love with Mary then he is not in a position to describe her as a gold-digging tart. (Well, one can dream up Dostoievskian exceptions to this point, but I concentrate on the typical case.) My description of Henry's beloved is a description from a perspective external to that of Henry. For a good phenomenological description (another matter) I should have to try to bring out what it is that Henry sees in Mary – to sketch in, so to say, the nimbus shimmering round her head, in Henry's vision of her. Naturally a lot of phenomenologically insensitive descriptions are not deliberately produced – they are 'unconscious' value-judgements, culture-bound slightings. To take a few examples: when images are called idols by Westerners; when uses are made of terms like 'animism' of African beliefs; and witch-doctors are called 'witch-doctors'. The other man's religion is, as we know, a superstition. The preceding arguments, then, add up to saying that it is not possible for the worshipper seriously to affirm that what he worships is merely a block of stone, even though the outsider may in critical vein want to assert this. The latter assertion is, however, properly a misdescription (the problem of whether misdescriptions can be valuable in the armoury of social and religious criticism is quite a different one from those which I am here considering). The perspective, though, of the outsider *is* secondary. It leaves untouched the basic and general point that to understand worshipping an image, one needs to grasp that there is a phenomenological object very inadequately described as a block of stone. That is, to understand the 'bowing down' one needs to grasp that there is a focus. That there is one only? To this issue we must return in due course.

1.14. *A comment arising about the scientific study of religion.* The remarks in the foregoing paragraph indicate why it is that the 'scientific' study of religion can often seem to be deflationary and indeed insensitive (for after all, if the objective is to be objective about religion, why be slighting about it all the time by extra-perspectival judgements?). The frequent neglect of the actors' perspective and so of the meaning of the phenomenological focus of their activities and sentiments is one of the ways in which the 'scientific' study fails to be scientific. Though it is not my aim to go into the matter here, I believe that the fully rounded and effective study of religion must employ the method of phenomenology, namely the attempt to arrive at a sensitive understanding of the actors' standpoint. There is no special reason why the scientific study of religion, which is bound to have some effect on religion itself, just as the study of politics affects politics, and so on, should assume a wrongly menacing guise beyond the menaces to the believer implicit in employing (for instance) the historical method to reveal the historicity or otherwise of sacred revelation. Similarly some sociological writings, in describing rather flatly and from a superior stance, values that also need to be evoked, seems highly disturbing. (There are of course reasons why sociology will be somewhat disturbing in any case, but in the long run we should let the real grounds of disturbance show through rather than mask them with bad phenomenology which diverts the disturbance to other areas. We owe it to human beings at least to try to understand them.)

1.15. *But why not just stone?* However, though we have produced a rather long-winded argument for saying that from the inner perspective of the worshipper he does not just (or even) worship a block of stone, we are as yet very far from saying anything constructive as to *why* this is the case. A beginning is provided by the fact that the language of worship begins with the vocative. In worship one addresses the focus of worship. To address a lump of stone is already to have a concept of it which goes beyond the idea of it as a lump of stone. Children's books are instructive in this connection. You have a railway engine, for example, which has feelings, intentions and purposes, and which acts as a sort of person. Within the perspective of the child's book it is possible for the engine to be addressed because it is not conceived just as a railway engine. (Incidentally adult engine-drivers sometimes personify their engines, up to a point, but there might be some doubt about a driver's sanity if he seriously expected the engine to talk back, declare its love for him and so on.) In the fantasy, the engine has been invested with some of the attributes of personhood. But would it be right to think that this is what is happening in the case of the statue of Ganesh? Is it that the statue is invested with personhood, Ganesh for instance?

1.16. *A complication: multipresence.* The above account will not quite do, for there is no suggestion that Ganesh is as it were 'trapped' in this one statue. It is not his only body. It is characteristic of divine powers that they can be multipresent. For instance, the god Agni (Fire) is present in instances of fire, and more intensely in the sacrificial fire (also in the sun, etc.). There is a principle of power-identity running through the various manifestations of the divine power. The same can occur in the more 'artificial' case of ritual objects and ritual acts. Thus for example the one divine being can be manifested in a number of statues, and Christ can be present in many Eucharists. There may also be degrees of special presence. Thus those who make pilgrimages to Our Lady of Walsingham do not precisely believe that this is a different Madonna from that one who is the Mother of Jesus, but giving her a quasi-separate individuality, as Our Lady of Walsingham, is a mode of expressing special presence (compared with the mode in which the Madonna may be present in St Catherine of Siena Church, Birmingham). One may then sum up a typical situation in regard to a divine being, that he is *multipresent*, and present in varying degrees. To say that he is multipresent is not to say 'omnipresent'. Even where a God is omnipresent, he is specially multipresent.

1.17. *The problem of omnipresence.* An important aspect of the

11

omnipresence of God is that it means that wherever you are you can pray to him and he will be present to hear you. It is tempting to try to analyse the idea of omnipresence as a licence to pray at any time. However, treating it more 'ontologically', one comes to some problems. First, if God were present equally everywhere there would be no ground to treat one presence, e.g. in Christ, as more revelatory than anything else. Second, there is the difficulty of God's being present in evil entities. Both questions arise in connection with the story told about the Welsh philosopher Sir Henry Jones, when he was at Glasgow University. It is said that some doubted his Christian orthodoxy. His philosophy was neo-Hegelian. To test Sir Henry someone asked him 'Do you believe in the divinity of Christ?' Sir Henry replied with aplomb: 'Far be it from me to deny that any man is divine.' If a doctrine of omnipresence is going to be sustained, there must at least be degrees of presence and manifestation. However, there is another point to consider. In much religious thinking the universe (roughly the material universe) is a particular: it is not the class of everything that exists. Rather it is the cosmos. With such a conception the divine being can be partially identified with 'all this' – as in the *Upaniṣads*; or God can be seen as continuous creator and sustainer of the cosmos, 'lying behind' every part of it. This might be called 'God's general immanence'. This has to be distinguished from his particular immanence (such as his special activity in biblical history, his sacramental presence and so forth). Particular immanence involves special multipresence. So even where God is treated as being in some sense omnipresent, we can still refer to his multipresence. It is with the question of what this notion amounts to that we are here mainly concerned, and it is possible to treat God and gods on a par, in that both typically are manifested multipresently.

1.18. *Equal and unequal presence.* As we have noted, there may be inequalities of presence. Thus every body of water, in Hindu India, can be taken as the Ganges. But these are secondary Ganges: no one is going to make a pilgrimage to a stream in Madhya Pradesh when it is possible to go to bathe in the Ganges at Benares. It will be necessary to consider briefly why such inequalities occur, but the ensuing discussion will take place on the assumption that we can neglect inequalities. Briefly, the reason for such inequalities, though rather variegated, very often has to do with derivations. A derived event or entity partakes of the power of the original from which it is derived, but still the original has that power *par excellence*. Consider for instance the repetition of Christ's risen power in the Easter celebration with the original resurrection-event.

1.19. *Ganesh and some statues.* Suppose there are just a few statues of Ganesh, all equally sacred and valid. How is it that Ganesh is present specially in each of these? After all, Ganesh is not precisely like some kind of liquid – so that you can feed equal amounts into the statues. No, Ganesh is not divided up between them (though sometimes the analogy of dividing up is used in the mythic-ritual context). Ganesh can also be thought of as subsisting in a heavenly realm, but we shall leave this point on one side. What then are we to say about the 'special presence' phenomenon? Perhaps an analogy with paintings will be useful – an analogy which incidentally relates to the conception of kathenotheism evolved by Max Mueller. If there is a picture of the Ganges in my room, I can (so to speak) gaze across the river's waters. This does not mean that I am thinking of the painting as a kind of window – or rather of its frame as being the edges of a window, *through* which I am looking across the Ganges. (Maybe this helps to explain our impatience with those restaurants and bars which try to trick you with 'windows' looking on to the isle of Capri or the Rocky Mountains.) If I really thought of the picture-frame as a window I should be very puzzled by the fact that the neighbouring picture, of a girl in an English garden in the rain, did not connect up as to perspective or content with the picture of the Ganges. As it is, I accept that the two pictures belong to differing inner worlds of their own. All the perspectives of pictures in a gallery do not represent a single system. This is no doubt one reason for the importance of the frame in Western figurative art. Non-figurative canvases are often left unframed. In brief, *within* the context of the frame and of the mode of viewing, the perspective of the picture is accepted. In a similar way it is possible for the temple and the ritual used to constitute a frame within which the presence of Ganesh is accepted. It is not a question of his partly being here and partly being somewhere else. I remember going to a performance of *Oklahoma* when it had already been done over a thousand times in the U.K. You could see the actors wearily muttering cracks to each other between lines, and you

13

suddenly lost the perspective of a fresh beautiful morning in Oklahoma, and jumped outside the frame. Momentarily, this was over the thousandth time that a little brown maverick was winking its eye. The acceptance of the frame is, then, important. When people begin to ask questions like 'How can Christ be present in Monte Cassino and Little Rock at the same time?' it is a sign that the frames are breaking down. In brief, then, we can explain the equal presence of Ganesh in his several statues as involving a 'one-at-a-time' acceptance of Ganesh's presence within the ritual, temple frame.

1.20. *Further remarks on identification.* It is worth noting as well that the identification of the disparate is a common feature of religious claims – the entities, however, also having analogical resemblances in many cases. Thus Brahman is Atman; three Persons are united in the Trinity; all the gods are Síva; Síva, Visṇu and Brahmā are united in the one Being – and so on. It is not particularly important to explore the criteria of identification here; but I mention the matter as itself preparing an atmosphere in which the many real Ganeshes as presented in ritual frames are but one. Further, we have made reference earlier (1.16) to the principle of power-identity, which refuses to take nominalism seriously, but sees all fires as manifesting and containing the universal fire.

1.21. *Personhood.* We have argued that the image is invested with qualities of personhood when it is addressed in worship. It would be tempting to look upon the image as being the body of the god. However, we must note that the relation between body and mind seems to differ as between human and divine beings. For one thing it is not a one-to-one relation in the case of the god and his images, except within the frame, perhaps, in which the ritual occurs. Or to put it better: from within the frame Ganesh is wholly there, in body and mind, and there is no question of his being less there within one frame than he is within another. For within the frame the other frames are absent. So, then, there is equal presence of Ganesh. But the human being cannot get into this position. I cannot, as it were, magically multiply myself, body and all, so that I can be equally vigorous in playing cricket simultaneously in Ceylon, Philadelphia and Winchester. Another point to bear in mind is that men who worship statues of Ganesh know perfectly well that these statues have been fashioned by human craftsmen (by

14

themselves, maybe). The questions raised about images as the 'bodies' of Ganesh can be illuminated somewhat, by appealing again to the power-identity principle. Meanwhile, what has been established is that equal presence is a frame phenomenon. That is, with regard to equality, the notion of Ganesh's being wholly present within the frame gives an explanation. But it leaves over the question of how there can be many statues.

1.22. *An excursus on powers and likenesses.* Why should all cases of fire display Agni? Why should the sun be identical with Agni? The answer is simple, of course, and up to a point naïve. The answer is that one fire resembles another and the sun relevantly resembles fires here on earth. At the risk of repeating what I have tried to analyse elsewhere, let me go deeper into this feature of mythic-ritual thought. Accept the notion of power-identity, and you have the tendency of a power to leak over, as it were, into anything betraying the relevant likeness. By some action we may bring a fire into being and Fire is there, a minor miracle. Very often the operations of ritual supplement natural likenesses and analogies with new forms of relevant likeness. This is somewhat unrealistically counted magical while other uses of ritual on the same principle are counted as being religious. Let us begin with a ritual example, and one familiar to many readers of English. At the Last Supper Christ pronounced certain words, including 'This is my body' and 'This is my blood'. The greater part of the Christian tradition has supposed that by uttering these words he in effect transformed the substances he was distributing to the disciples. The fact that bread is solid and light-coloured and that wine is red and liquid is not irrelevant. It makes the new identity of bread and wine in the ritual circumstance 'natural'. That is, it latches on to an analogy between ordinary bread and wine and ordinary flesh and blood. There exists relevant likeness. Later re-enactments of the Last Supper also involve the transformation (however theologically excogitated) of the elements into the flesh and blood of the living Christ. And one reason why they manage this is that the re-enactments relevantly resemble the Last Supper: in a sense they mimic the action of Christ. However many intermediate steps may have occurred (e.g. the evolution of liturgy from something in upper rooms and houses to something in special edifices, with discs of unleavened bread and peculiar wine – not to mention all the changes effected by cultural transposition:

15

going into English, the fact that wine is not the natural drink of Englishmen, and so on), there nevertheless remains, or is thought to remain, a relevant likeness between the Eucharist or Mass now and the Last Supper itself. This is ritually relevant, for it is by the likeness that the power of the original event is transferred (there is thus an analogy to the case of natural forces: Agni manifests himself in fire here and now; Agni is the Original Fire – so to speak). In brief, then, in the Lord's Supper there is an underlying principle of the identity of like objects, so that they share power. In this way the Eucharist shares the power of the (first) Last Supper.

1.23. *An interruption about inequalities*. We had assumed in the earlier discussion (1.18) that Ganesh is equally present in the various images. But we did also advert to the fact that in a lot of cases there is unequal distribution of the one power (e.g. over the question of the Ganges and other bodies of water in the Indian subcontinent). The discussion in the preceding paragraph illuminates one inequality. Though the power of Christ is fully present in the Eucharist (hence the doctrines of Real Presence and its counterparts), there is a difference between Sunday morning's Eucharist and the first Last Supper. The difference is that next Sunday morning's Eucharist is not a foundational event. It does not authorise Christ's action, but Christ's action authorises it. How are we to look upon this asymmetry? What does authorisation consist of in the context under discussion, and more generally in the complexes of myth and ritual? It is not as though Christ was elected to do something. But he was believed, or later it came about that he was believed, to have divine power; and this implies the possibility of giving over that power, graciously. I say 'graciously' for the following set of reasons.

1.24. *Keeping the status quo in ritual*. A man salutes his chief. For instance he touches his forelock. Why does he do it? Out of deference as we say. But what would happen if he didn't? If he didn't just in a dumb way, the chief would tend to get angry and throw his weight around. He would blast him verbally, say (and what is it to do *that*? Isn't the power of words very amazing? Precisely so). But if the man made his not touching his forelock into a counter-thing, a counter-ritual, like cocking a snook, then the chief's actions might be even more violent. Why is all this? It is surely not because the chief is just arrogant and the man

16

insufficiently subservient, though these remarks may well be true. The chief may in his way be a very nice person, gentle normally and courteous. The point is that he conceives himself as chief, is chief, and plays that role convincedly. Thus he wishes to maintain the *status quo*. This is one in which he has more power than his underling. This power is conserved and to some extent sustained by the rituals which he exchanges with his underling. The touch on the underling's forelock is an act which is a sign of inferior power and status. In being a sign it is not a mere symbol, a mere gesture. It is a realisation of the inferiority. It manifests it. It is part of it. Thus any refusal to touch the forelock becomes itself a charged event. On the principle of likeness (like beings share the same power), if the chief and his underling give like salutations to one another and treat each other as fully alike, then they share the same power. But in fact they do not. Any ritual or counter-ritual which signifies that they do is itself a diminution of power. Thus the man who does not touch his forelock is not merely not recognising by gesture the superior status of the chief: he is actually threatening that status. More, he has diminished it a bit. So the chief reacts to restore the *status quo*. Normally he would acknowledge the salute of his underling, which was a kind of reinforcement of the other's attribution of his power. But he cannot maintain the *status quo* by simply grinning or acknowledging the lack of salutation by the other. His power being ritually diminished, the ritual response must be one in which the inferiority of the other is increased. Hence the reaction of verbal blasting (for instance) which is a ritual cursing, or something like that, of the other. If the other takes it, then he has sacrificed the peaceful acknowledgement from his chief (itself recognising and conferring status even if it be inferior). So his ritual 'account' has been debited, to make up for his attempt to increase his ritual power-balance by 'getting above himself' as it is sometimes called. The ritual, then, of subservience on the part of the underling is part of the subservience; and the ritual of effortless superiority likewise is part of the power of the chief.

1.25. *Grace and the power system.* As I have rather crudely described the power system as expressed in signs between a chief and his underling, I have relied on the secret principle that unlikenesses cause unlikenesses. Or rather I have implicitly appealed to what follows from the principles of power-identity

17

and of likeness. If X is like Y, then the power of X is found in Y. If someone tries to make Z like Y, then the power of X will be found in Z unless something is done about it. The action of the chief described in the preceding paragraph is a way of doing something about it; because the unlike act will produce the unlike result. Thus if I wear some sign, such as fine clothing, which makes me unlike the masses, then this act as it were 'repels' the masses. The possessor of one sort of power will try to conserve it by signalising his difference from other people (classes of people); for if they were to become like him then his power would leak over into them. Thus one of superior status, such as a king, has to be gracious when he transmits his power to underlings. He may need to transmit, for practical and other reasons: let us not here enter into this side of the problem (one essentially of the limitations of power). But if he simply lets other folk come close to him, become like him and so on, then his power-substance will leak away. He therefore has to transfer power to his underlings on a certain condition which he makes plain by his behaviour – his ritual actions. The despot is capricious, and his capriciousness is not essentially a matter of character. It is itself a ritual sign that others lie below him, have no grip upon him, are unlike him and so on. Where the ritual of the king–underling relationship is such that the latter has rights, in other words powers, eating into the chief's, then these powers are acknowledged in a regular manner by the chief. But where he maintains his own power without conceding parts of it, his delegations must take a capricious, non-ritual (though in a way ritual) form. That is, they must have an aspect of irregularity, and must not be 'ritualistic', replete with regular ceremony. For the capriciousness is ritual in being a sign; but it is not ritualistic, in being a regular sign. Thus what power may be conferred by the absolute despot is uncannily uncertain. It is a matter of grace rather than rights; of favour rather than rights; of caprice rather than rituals. Such despotic caprice is of course rather rare. But I hope I have succeeded in bringing out something of the logic of ritual which is relevant to the notion of worship. For as will readily be seen (and it is a point to which we are bound to come back in due course), there is an application to the logic of worship and of grace in religion.

1.26. *Authority, grace, inequality.* The present discussion arises out of an attempt to understand something about the authority connected with foundational events, such as the Last Supper. Though Christ selected bread and wine – substances having a certain natural resemblance to flesh and blood – no one was compelled to equate the two pairs of substances. The equation is a result of a one-sided act, in which Christ, in deeming these entities equivalent, in the appropriate ritual circumstance, to his own substance, confers his own power upon them. Questions then of power-identity and resemblance can be approached from two directions. On the one hand men may be seeing resemblance between a cult object or ritual event and some natural power enter into relationship with that power, hoping to turn it to their advantage. On the other hand, in the case of the despotic power, the resemblance can arise from the opposite direction. Thus God did not need to create. It was a fiat. But in creating man he conferred some of his own substance upon him, namely he 'made man in his own image'. Similarly Christ confers Christ-likeness upon those who follow him. But let us note what is required of men in such a context. It is not that men should perform works of a moral sort (this is the fruit of faith), but rather that they should acknowledge God and Christ. What is it to acknowledge them? It is to perform an act of acknowledgement, itself a ritual in effect (though later we need to look at one or two problems in connection between rituals and mental dispositions, etc.). The words 'Thou art my Lord and King' signalise my difference from God – my inferiority, his superiority. I am at the same time recognising that God is the sole source of holiness, of that substance by which I am saved. Paradoxically, it is by an act which helps to conserve that holy power, so that it does not 'leak across' the boundary between the divine and human, that the situation is prepared where that power can freely cross the boundary, through the act of God. Thus in this second mode of resemblance, the likeness on the human side is conferred graciously by God. *Hubris*, pride, sin – these are ways in which there is not proper acknowledgement of the unique supremacy and power of the divine. The latter is like the chief whose chieftainship is not acknowledged by the underling. Some punitive ritual from the divine side is needed in order to redress the infringed *status quo*.

1.27. *Other foundations.* The above account of the reason for the superiority of Christ himself and of the foundational Last Supper over later Eucharists, in which also Christ is of course

19

present, should not lead us to neglect another reason for the superiority of the 'once-upon-a-time' events of mythic-ritual complexes. As has been well brought out by Eliade, among others, many rituals are themselves representations of great events in *illud tempus*, mythic time. The fact that a ritual now is a re-presentation of a prototypical event gives the latter value-priority. But this leads us to consider the function of myth itself. Let us do so by returning to the question of Ganesh and his images.

1.28. *Image and myth.* It is obvious enough that Ganesh's images have a practical rather than a contemplative significance. They were not shaped for the sake of the Metropolitan Museum. Ganesh's presence in the images is acknowledged in ritual and by saluting the god; we feel his substance (just as the salute of the underling to the chief is part of the chief's power). Reciprocally the god may confer some favour upon the worshipper, such as good fortune in some business transaction. But Ganesh's power is related to his nature and past deeds, that is it is related to the myths which are represented and celebrated in the ritual surrounding him. Thus it is not wise to look upon the image as a simple object: rather it maintains its life in the rituals going on before it. One could put this by saying that just as Ganesh is equally present in his different images, so he is equally present in the ritual re-enactments of his life before each image. This helps to explain one way in which Ganesh transcends his images. In the first place he is not just a block of stone but is endowed with personal characteristics as seen by the way in which he is addressed. Second, his life in 'another time' is re-presented in connection with the image. Thus he, like a human, is not just his body, but the one you see before you has both mind and biography.

1.29. *Dynamics of superiority.* However, we have been chiefly concerned to elucidate the concept of worship, and some of the ceremonies may not be so directly worship as others (the point we can illustrate from some forms of Christian worship: thus some services called 'Morning Worship' or the like include readings from the Bible, and reading from the Bible is not *per se* a form of worship directly, though it acquires an aspect of worship through the context of the service). Taking the worship of Ganesh in its most 'primitive' form, it involves bowing down as a ritual act directed to Ganesh as focus, who is addressed. What

20

more precisely does the bowing down signify? As is readily apparent from a cursory inspection of our own and many other languages and from the symbolisms of many cultures, up is superior, down is inferior – it is ironic that one has to explain the matter by using the latinised words that merely signify 'upper' and 'lower'. The act of worship includes bowing down to symbolise the inferiority of the worshipper to the focus of worship. Now of course not all cases of expressing inferiority are cases of worship – men bow down before potentates, holy men and so on. To say that the worshipper is ascribing higher value to the focus than to himself is to say something, but there are different modes of value. Incidentally it is not to the point to counter-argue with instances of where the god is, by moral or other criteria, inferior to his devotees, for this is to make a value-judgement from a different perspective, like the earlier cases which we have discussed.

1.30. *How would one distinguish worship from other symbolisms of inferiority?* One way of trying to bring out the particular mode of value which is expressed in the practice of worship – *this* sort of bowing down – is to look to the sentiments involved. This in part was what was done by Rudolf Otto in his famous description of the numinous. In talking of the *mysterium tremendum et fascinans* he was adverting to sentiments of fear and (by fascination) exaltation. But of course he had to show what sort of fear is involved. This he did by citing a number of examples of uncanny and holy fear. Perhaps in English the word 'awe' is the best one to indicate the sentiment which worship expresses and which ritual also evokes. So the superiority of the focus of worship would then become one which is awe-inspiring. But this by itself would not succeed in differentiating between worship and bowing down before Louis Quatorze – he was awe-inspiring to many of his courtiers. One could pose the connection: What extra difference does it make when the king is conceived as divine (like the Pharaoh)? What differentiates the sentiments directed at Louis Quatorze from those directed towards Amenhotep IV? For Otto presumably it would be that the sentiments directed towards the latter would involve feeling the numinous – and this experience, the *sensus numinis*, is held by him to be *sui generis* (in effect its presence becomes the defining characteristic of religion). The theophany of Krishna in the *Bhagavadgita*, the vision of Isaiah in the Temple – such experiences are prime examples of the numinous. It is very hard, however, properly to delineate a range of objects in terms of the sentiments which they arouse, especially if the sentiment in question is both *sui generis* and at the same time subtly similar to other experiences (of ghosts, the uncanny in general). Can one on the basis of the account in Otto be sure that an H-bomb explosion would not give rise to the sense of the numinous? Despite such difficulties, I think Otto has managed to delineate a range of experiences by examples. He is wrong in thinking that the numinous is in effect definitory of the rel gious: for instance, the highest experience for some religions is contemplative, as in the practice of *dhyāna* in Buddhism – Theravada Buddhism is a case where the *central* value is not properly described in terms of either the numinous or the Holy. (But the question is complex: I am far from denying that Sinhalese peasants worship gods and pay tribute to the Buddha who is better than the gods – do they then worship the Buddha and is he numinous for them? Opinions differ. In theory he is not a god; in practice . . .? These ambiguities keep striking us in the history of religion: Mexican saints, the Madonna in Italy – are these in effect gods?)

1.31. *A diversion towards the Buddha.* Perhaps some light can be thrown by the example of the cult of the Buddha in the Theravada. At least it may help to differentiate *within* religion between an object of worship and the object of something else. Let us briefly recapitulate the situation there and a problem. By the way, I am thinking here of Buddhism in Ceylon: not all the remarks I make may be fully applicable to Theravada Buddhism elsewhere, for example in Thailand. The situation, very crudely, is as follows: that though there are Buddha images in temples before which the faithful lay flowers and the like, the doctrine precludes us from saying that people worship the Buddha. We shall see why in a moment. But meanwhile it is also true that the faithful worship such gods as Vishnu and Kataragama in shrines typically part of the complex of which the image-house is part. Further, according to the doctrine, and one could reasonably claim according to the ordinary adherent, the Buddha is superior to the gods. Thus though there is a cult of a Buddha who is higher than the gods, this cult is not properly one of worship. This is a mildly perplexing state of affairs. Let us first see, however, why it is that the doctrine denies that

22

there can be worship of the Buddha. The reason has to do with the famous 'undetermined' question as to whether a Tathagata (i.e. the Buddha) can be said to exist after his final decease, that is after his passing away in a state of liberation. The scriptures compare the question to the question of where a fire or flame goes when it goes out. The question is wrongly posed, in the deepest possible way, so that it is neither right to say that the Tathagata survives, nor that he does not, nor that he both does and does not, nor that he neither does nor does not. A formidable series of negations. Why should the question be malformed? Briefly, because of the Buddhist metaphysics. An individual consists in a congeries of short-lived events of different types. When these are, so to say, dispersed, there is no individual to refer to, either as existing or as not existing and so on. Thus it is with the Buddha, for the individuality of Gautama is dispersed through his having attained *nirvana*. This being so, there is no Buddha 'out there' who can be worshipped. There is no individual focus of piety with whom there can be any transactions. Hence the doctrine considers the cult of images as being a means of revering the memory of the deceased teacher. Yet in some way the Buddha is more 'powerful' than the gods, who *are* in some sense 'out there' and to be encountered in transactions. This has to be understood in connection with the problem of what is the central value of Theravada Buddhism. This is *nirvana* – that state in which there is complete serenity and insight and which constitutes liberation from the otherwise unending round of rebirth. Is it sensible to say that this, *nirvana*, is a focus of worship? Is it the Buddhist equivalent of the Godhead? It is not, for the following reasons. First, *nirvana* is a state of the individual, rather than an entity or being (those who deny that God is *a* being still count him as the ground, or as being itself, rather than as a state). Of course what I have just said about *nirvana* is awkwardly put, for the state is one which leads to the disappearance of the individual. But let us put it this way: that the stream of events constituting Ananda is replaced ultimately by a state in which there is no longer any Ananda to be reborn. Thus logically the concept of *nirvana* is more like that of liberation than it is like that of Lord. For one cannot sensibly ask whether there is one *nirvana* (there is, however, maybe, one mode of attaining it); but it is quite in order to ask whether there is but one Lord (for which reason

23

there is some distance between the ordinary notion of God and the sophisticated – if it be so – idea of God as being rather than as *a* being). Of course it may later become possible to use *nirvana* in a different way, where it becomes identified with the Absolute (*Tathatā* and so on) – a usage perhaps rather similar in form to 'God is love'. But generally speaking, in the Theravada at least, *nirvana* is not a single 'thing' or 'non-thing'. Second, even if it were so thought of, it is not personal: it is a refuge, a haven, an immortal place – but it is not a personal Being with whom one could enter into transactions, as with the gods. Third, *nirvana* is a state accruing upon the practice of meditation rather than worship.

1.32. *Meditation versus worship*. The last point implies a radical separation which needs backing. I would not deny that people can meditate upon an object of worship and that they can regard such meditation as being a kind of worship. How could this be denied if the earlier account of the superimposition of the category of worship upon other tasks, such as sweeping a room, is correct? But I should want to argue that one can meditate (contemplate) and indeed attain to mystical states without worshipping. In other words, though meditation is a central part of the life of some religions and religious movements, it is not to be identified with worship *tout court* – for which reason it is not possible to define religion in terms of worship. What then is the difference between meditation and worship? First, no ritual need be involved in contemplation (though this is perhaps a tricky point to sustain, in that certain external acts, such as adopting a posture and, say, closing one's eyes, may be part of the business of contemplating). Second, the practice of, for example, the stages of meditation (*jhānas*) in Theravada Buddhism aims at emptying the mind of discursive thoughts, such as the thought of an object of worship. That is, the set-up precludes the relevant intentionality. Third, the state of liberation which is aimed at in some systems of yoga, including Theravadinyoga, does not involve any idea of 'being close' to God or any other object of worship. Thus it is not surprising that Theravada Buddhism and Sankhya-Yoga have very weak notions of god and do not believe in a Creator of the universe. Their sights are fixed on a different type of supreme value. It may be noted that just as meditation can be seen under the guise of worship, where it occurs in a theistic context, so God

24

can be seen as little more than a useful device for achieving purity of consciousness: thus the Lord in the Yoga system serves as a useful model to meditate upon, but does not actually bring about the liberation of those who may meditate upon him. Thus we may work, rather crudely, with a distinction between meditation (mysticism) and worship. It is a distinction which brings out the fact that in Theravada Buddhism the one activity is prized much more highly than the other. Though Buddhism does not deny or destroy the gods, the path to freedom does not lie along the path of devotion, numinosity and piety, but rather along the eightfold path which culminates in the higher contemplative states of *samādhi*. The Buddha as teacher is important precisely because he points us along this way, and thus saves us indirectly, by giving us the prescription which we can translate into a powerful medicine in our own lives.

1.33. *Superiority and numinosity*. It is now possible to understand the state of affairs surrounding the cult of the Buddha in Theravada Buddhism in the following way. The Buddha is higher than the gods, but not on a line extended from within the scale of gods. That is, he is of greater value, but not of greater *numinous* value. Of course, it can look that way, for the flavour of the numinous can still cling to that which transcends the numinous. But strictly, the Buddha belongs to a different category. His essence is related, so to say, to the practice of meditation and the goal of *nirvana*, not to the whole practice of worship. Thus the Theravada transcends polytheism, but not in the direction of one Lord infinitely more powerful and holy than the lesser gods. In brief, it is necessary to distinguish differing kinds of superiority. The ritual expression of superior/ inferior status in worship is more akin to the social rituals of inferiority, etc. We shall be returning to this point later. Meanwhile we may note a slightly differing situation regarding the superiority of the contemplative goal in Advaita and in Mahayana Buddhism, which is worth a brief discussion.

1.34. *Two levels in the religious ultimate*. In Advaita Vedanta, as is well known, Brahman can be treated on two levels. According to the higher truth, there is only 'one without a second', Brahman, without personal attributes, but made up somehow of reality, consciousness and bliss. With this we are in our essential nature identical. The existential realisation of this

25

identity is in effect liberation. But at a lower level, Brahman can be treated as the Creator and focus of worship. It is a lower level, because the Creator shares the illusoriness of the world which he supposedly creates. He is part of *māyā*. From a practical point of view all this means that we can worship God so long as we are not in that higher state where we realise liberation and know that there is no Other to worship. This doubledecker doctrine is parallel to that of the Madhyamika school of Mahayana Buddhism, only there it is not Brahman that is ultimate but the Void. It is not Śiva or Viṣṇu that is worshipped but rather heavenly Buddhas and Bodhisattvas who are such powerful influences in helping living beings. But they vanish ultimately in the dazzling darkness of the Void, and begin to take on the guise, in recollection, of a fiction useful in luring the faithful on to a higher view. All this came to be systematised in the doctrine of the three bodies of the Buddha – the different aspects, as we might better call them, of Buddhahood, the highest of which is identical with the Void and with the liberated state. In both these systems one can note a divergence from the Theravada, namely that there is a sort of 'thing' or 'non-thing' lying beyond the object of worship. As Otto has pointed out, we can find a similar conception in Eckhart's distinction between Godhead and God. But what, from our point of view, is significant in the contrast with the Theravada is that there is more directly a sense in which the pious worship the Ultimate, for the Ultimate and God are held in some sense to be identical, though they exist at different levels. However, the transactional aspect of worship comes out here too; for when one realises one's identity with Brahman one sees that there can be no Other into relationship with whom one can enter. Though it is not appropriate to go into the matter here, I believe that the two-level ontology has its roots in a synthesis between the practice of meditation and the activity of worship, both being valued, but the former much more than the latter. By contrast original Theravada Buddhism had little place for worship (sacrifice, etc.) and there was no need to link very strongly the object or objects of worship and related rituals to the goal of the contemplative life.

1.35. *A summary of the discussion of worship.* So far the arguments which I have been pursuing seem to yield the following conclusions. First, worship is a relational activity: one cannot worship oneself, as in the famous joke about the typical Englishman, who is a self-made man who worships his maker. Second, the ritual of worship expresses the superiority of the Focus to the worshipper(s). Third, the ritual also performatively sustains or is part of the power of the Focus. Fourth, the experience which worship expresses is that of the numinous, and the object of worship is thus perceived as awe-inspiring.

1.36. *An interlude on the language of worship.* These features of worship can be brought out by looking at some aspects of the language of worship. First, consider those utterances in worship which do not *say* anything: such as the chant 'Holy, holy, holy, Lord God of Sabaoth'. To say 'Holy' is not to describe anything (though if it is uttered with sincerity the utterer will also doubtless believe that 'God is holy' states some kind of truth). It is, however, ascribing holiness to the Focus, and thus is properly used in addressing him. Of course, very often people use such utterances out of context, in a blasphemous or half-blasphemous way, as in the use of the oath 'My God', which is not addressed to God, but somehow mimics the addressing situation. Provided that one uses a term like 'Holy' and addresses it correctly, one can then worship without stating anything. Why then do hymns and prayers so often go on to say things about God? Things, moreover, which are usually very well known to the hearers and presumably also to the Lord. The reason lies in the performative character even of these descriptions; for their function is celebratory. In telling God at Easter that he has raised his Son up from the dead, the worshipper is not reminding God or the congregation, but re-presenting the event. Thus as a general observation it is roughly true to say that stating descriptions is not a primary aspect of any worship. Indeed if the account here given is correct, the question of truth has a very different significance from usual. If a hymn or liturgy re-enacts some primary sacred event, and does so in part by the use of words, the role of those words is to mimic the original. The power which they possess lies in their resemblance to the original in crucial respects. By the principle of likeness referred to earlier (1.16) they come to share in the power of the primary event and thus their use in the celebration reactivates the power of the primary event. All this is, of course, not to deny that it can prove embarrassing if the words descriptively are not *true*. This is one reason why historical inquiry into primary religious events can so often be thought by the faithful to be dangerous and blasphemous, because it threatens the celebrations, and so in a way may promise the subtraction of some of God's power.

1.37. *Worship and the ineffable.* As Otto pointed out, silence can also be used in worship and can indeed be the most effective way of conveying the supreme holiness of God. Note, however, that we need to contextualise silences, as there are different varieties. A sacred hush succeeding the singing of 'Holy, holy, holy' serves to express holiness. This is not the same as the silence, for instance, of the Buddha about the topics of the undetermined questions, for the Buddha was not intending to worship, or to ascribe praise to a supreme Being. We may note also that the silence of worship is possibly complex in its significance. For, firstly, it is itself an element in a flow of speech-acts, and to that extent can count as a verbal gesture (then there are questions of how well or ill this gesture can be used to express the solemnity of the rite, etc.). Secondly, it can be a mimicking of something about the nature of God, namely that no words can convey his supreme holiness. 'No words can convey . . .' – but what does this mean? Note that we often use this very expression in order to convey something, for instance our deep gratitude to someone. It is surely not right to think that the trouble arises from a lack, say, of technical vocabulary. How can there be a limit on description of that which is already admitted to be somewhat describable? (For it is not feasible to take the heroic path of saying that God is totally indefinable and indescribable; for then why use the term 'God', and what would there be to believe in anyway? Such a 'being' would have no purchase at all upon reality.) The trouble which 'No words can convey . . .' conveys is of a different order, and can be put very crudely in the following way. Consider pains: they are more or less intense (I neglect differences in quality), and can be expressed appropriately by more or less intense expressions. But somehow the conventions get broken through by a really horrible pain, and our ouches are quite inadequate. This is where a pain of great intensity can properly be expressed by the expression 'indescribable'. Similarly with the unspeakable gifts of God. Thus the sentence 'Thou art indescribably great' succeeds in expressing intensely the great greatness of God. Thus silence can be a nobler and more effective expression of worship than a lot of attempts to babble expressive language. It is, incidentally,

28

interesting how expressive language gets devalued – there is a sort of continual inflation, which has to be combated by inventing new expressions. Once upon a time the adverb 'excruciatingly' did a strong job in front of 'funny' – but now it has become a cliché, worn down, robbed of its old substance. One protection against this inflation is to retain a mysterious, rather unintelligible language. One of the reasons for sacred languages in religion is precisely their power to remain beyond the cliché. Consider how even in modern Christianity, which has gone over mostly to vernacular liturgies, there remain certain foreign and ancient words embedded in prayer and worship: Amen, Lord God of Sabaoth, Alleluia, etc.

1.38. *Meditation and the ineffable.* As has been pointed out above, there are different varieties of silence. Thus the sophisticated use of riddles (koans) in Zen is designed to break down conceptual thinking in the interests of reaching pure experience, and is connected therefore with the idea that silence 'conveys' well the nature of reality (for words do not, being the vehicles, so to say, of concepts). Again, the negative theology of Pseudo-Dionysius has much to do with the mystical, interior quest which in later times also stressed the way in which the Truth lies beyond words. Part of the explanation is the same as that given above, but with a differing application. That is, the mystical experience is so blissful (to use a weak word) that to express it one must go off the top of the word-scale and call it ineffable. The difference of application lies in the fact that here it is the expression of joy, bliss or what have you that is in view, not the expression of divine superiority in the situation of praise. Another reason is that the mystical experience neither involves external perception nor internal images. It thus cannot be described in the literal sense of 'describe' – I cannot say things like 'It is a red dragon on a tall mountain that I see in my mind's eye'. The two main points here are, indeed, combined in the Zen notion of breaking down concepts, and in the idea of certain things lying beyond understanding. Thus it would seem that the mystical silence differs from the silence of worship. But, of course, the two can coalesce, as we have seen more than once, because of the possibility of thinking of the one Reality as being approachable in the two ways, of worship and meditation. The silence itself can serve as a kind of cement, and perhaps even in part as a ground for the coalescence. However, the main point

29

which I wish to make is that there is no necessary identification of the two sorts of silence, and this therefore is one way in which it is important to contextualise silence, as we have argued above.

1.39. *Not just silence: other aspects of contexts.* So far we have looked at context in rather a general way. As regards worship it is not only the non-words of silence that need to be given context, but also the words of praise. That is, the 'Holy, holy, holy' typically is uttered in a certain milieu, and in a certain way. The tone of voice, even, can be important. Thus it has now become quite a common event for forms of worship to be transposed into a secular setting where the context no longer really holds. Thus a celebrated musical Mass gets performed as a concert piece, just as an image may be treated as a work of art in a museum. It is naturally possible for these things to occur, because if one assembles cultural objects (whether sculptures or cantatas) for one purpose, they can always be disassembled: the statue taken from the temple, the music from the rite and so on. There is nothing disgraceful about such disassembling as such, but we need to raise the question of what kind of change occurs as between settings? Is it just that the intentions are different? That is, is it that on the one hand in a sacred setting the choral Mass is a case of worship, for it is intended in this way, while on the other hand in the concert hall the performance is simply a recital, because that is the way it is seen by the participants? Obviously one can think of cases where the mere intention makes the difference (like my singing a hymn in my bath: is it praise? Well, it is if that is the way I mean it: but conversely it could be just a song to sing in a bath, a mindless piece of unsacred exuberance). But it would be unwise to neglect the primary role of ritual. Suppose the Mass was enacted in the Albert Hall according to Roman rites, with someone either being or acting the part of the celebrant and so on. What would we say? The very ritual setting would induce different questions from those induced by a setting of choirs and a conductor, etc. It might turn out to be a sort of play-acting (but consider the complications: people taking Communion and the priest a mere actor . . .); but it would be the play-acting of a ritual Mass, not the play-acting of a choral occasion. Hence typically the right context which makes the words 'Holy, holy, holy' worshipful is the ritual one. This, in other words, is what makes us look on those words as being part of the whole rite.

30

1.40. *The performative and commitment*. The above account reinforces the general observation of the centrally performative role of language in worship. To be committed to worship is to be involved in a religion, but it is worth remarking that the self-involvement may go very deeply into the moral (political, etc.) sphere, inasmuch as the religion contains a strong ethical dimension. This of course harks back to our earlier idea of 'superimposition'. But the transaction with God in worship, etc., may include commitments (freely entered into, if he is very powerful and good) on his part. The exploration of all this is well done in Donald Evans's *The Logic of Self-Involvement*. If there is a problem about the book, it is that the 'factual', descriptive side of belief is left a bit tenuous, so that it is hard to know how much in the way of such beliefs is a necessary condition of commitment (worship, etc.). A similar problem arises in regard to Existentialist accounts of Christian faith. This leads us back to the definition of the gods. Can they be defined by our sentiments or ritual attitudes? This is one version of the same general humanising perspective, which may run counter to the grain of realism in both commonsense and scientific philosophy.

1.41. *Numinosity and the gods again*. It was suggested earlier (1.30) that the numinous experience is in a sense definitive of worship: and this might hint that it was definitive of the gods, if the latter turn out after all to be the kind of being that one worships (that is, if they turn out to be in effect defined in this way). I think that it is indeed feasible to define the gods thus, but this does not mean that the gods depend on us for their existence, despite rumours to the contrary. The rumours suppose that the gods are human projections. Feuerbach, Marx, Peter Berger and others foster these rumours. I would not wish to deny that they are advancing theses which may end up proved or at least highly plausible, with plenty of evidence on their side. But the projectionist theses are also hypo-; and they express contingencies. After all, the idea of a god is not the idea of a projection (though some Buddhists get near to saying this). The idea of a god is of a being who would exist even if human beings did not. Nevertheless a god is relational, as is witnessed by such locutions as 'My God, my God, why hast thou forsaken me?' or 'His God is Viṣṇu'. Why 'his'? Why 'my'? Precisely because the concept of God or a god is relational – like *uncle*. One might therefore want to say that if all human beings and other worshipping creatures were to be wiped out there would be no God or gods, just as if all my nephews get killed I am no longer an uncle. The gods, though, or God would still exist, would they not? Thus it may well be possible to *define* God or gods in terms of worship (or in terms of the numinous experience) without 'humanising' or subjectivising them. There would of course remain a question about the nature of the gods' separate existence 'in themselves' as we might say. What properties does a god have other than being a proper object of worship (typically, that is – we must still keep in mind the *dei otiosi*)? And what properties do gods have other than numinosity? But it might be objected that the latter question has a different status from the former. Let us consider why this might be so.

1.42. *Ritual versus experience.* It could be argued that the numinous experience gives as it were information about the gods, so that to define the gods as being the objects of numinous experience would say something or other about their character (for instance that they are mysterious, awe-inspiring and of course fascinating). This was what Otto was after: a 'realism of religious experience', an analogue to perception in the spiritual sphere. This was a worthy and intelligible goal, and it puts the gods on quite a different footing from the relational idea set out in the preceding paragraph. However, it might be pointed out that mysteries are mysteries for someone. And someone has to be inspired with awe. And then again someone has to be fascinated. I put the matter a bit imprecisely of course; but the point is that the description of the numinous makes out that it reveals powers in the object, and these powers are to be defined relationally. It therefore follows that the concept of the numinous is quite as relational as the concept of object of worship, only it turns out that it is relational in a more secret way. The distinction between the two cases, then, turns out to be a fraud. Still, experiences have content, and the blues and greens and reds which colour the objects of our world can by the same argument be thought to be merely the results of the powers of objects. Let us look at them in this way: we yet consider that there is a sense in which the greens which we experience tell us something about the objects which are green. They are green, not just greening, we might say. There is, we feel, a more intrinsic connection between experience and the

32

way things are than between action and the way things are. If I kneel before a block of stone, that does not tell us much or anything about the stone. But if I see it is grey (or think I see it is grey), then there is an inclination to make at least one specific judgement about the stone. Some such reasons may lead us to look upon experience as a better basis for the definition of the gods than ritual, even though at the back of our minds there lurks the uneasy philosophical suspicion that greens and greys are as relational as unclehood, not to mention nephewness. From the point of view, however, of the present argument, the concept of the numinous plays a particular role; for it helps us to differentiate between merely social rituals and those which concern the gods. So, then, we wish to define the gods relationally as the recipients of worship, namely the kind of ritual which expresses the numinous. The gods are, in brief, holy.

1.43. *The way in which the gods transcend the relational.* As we have argued, it would be somewhat absurd simply to suppose that the gods depend on us (that is, the gods considered phenomenologically – the theory that we invented them has very little to do with the way in which we pray to them and look upon them as existing 'out there'). If we return to the model of the uncle and the nephew: the uncle exists in his own right, however much he may be defined by the relationship. In what way does the god exist in his own right? And how far does he retain his status once the ritual has decayed or disappeared? Consider Agni, for example. We have earlier made out that Agni is present really in cases of fire and in the sun and so forth. He is also present, as we have seen, in his images. He also transcends all this, in the stories of his exploits – or rather in the events, or supposed events, of which the mythic stories are a reflection and likeness and therefore a part (by the principle of likeness and all that). Now the sun and fire and so forth are not actually created by the ritual: they exist and are taken as objects of ritual, in the collage which the myth-ritual maker makes his own. A different account of course would need to be given in regard to the one God of Israel or Christianity. For instance, the one God is manifest (in a sense) not so much in fire – a particular substance – as in the cosmos considered as a unified whole. This manifestation owes something to ideas of nature in the last two or three hundred years of Western culture. But in addition to his presence there, the one God is present in the narrow circum-

33

stances of the Mass as a re-creation in part of what became manifest in a particular stretch of history in ancient Palestine. There is in brief a necessary particularity (even the particularity of the one cosmos or universe) in the one God. This must put him epistemologically and in principle ontologically with the lesser gods, which are also highly particular. So we get to the position: every god reveals himself in particular circumstances to the human world, and expects the ritual which feeds his substance. But every god is also 'beyond' his particular manifestations and exists as more than a mere object of ritual or human experience. This does not prevent us from *defining* the gods relationally (as we have noted above – 1.42). But we still want to know more about the ontological status of gods in so far as they are not constituted by the relationship. Or rather, in what way do the gods transcend those particularities through which they manifest themselves?

1.44. *The invisibility of gods.* The gods may manifest themselves in images and acts, but they are for all that in some respect invisible. It may be that the investigation of this will throw light on the manner in which the gods transcend their manifestations. But as would be expected, the situation is complicated. For the invisibility of the gods is much more heavily stressed in some religions than others. Consider Judaism, Islam and some forms of the Christian tradition, where images are barred. Let us clear out of the way a problem which we left on one side much earlier in the discussion – namely, how you bow down before a god who is not located in a statue or other manifestation?

1.45. *The direction where god is.* The matter of bowing down to the one God is especially strange because of his omnipresence. Any old direction would do, and yet by the same token every bowing towards would be a bowing away from. In one connection, the thesis that any old direction will do complements the thesis that any old place will do; and this is an important and correct statement, for it indicates that one is never left alone by God and that one can pray to him in any place one is. Hence there is an infinite possibility of the practice of the presence of God. This is one main point indeed of the doctrine of omnipresence (there are some other points as well – for instance that God is continuously the creator and preserver of all things, including, alas, the bad things; but we do not here need to get embroiled in the problem of evil). Nevertheless, though we may

34

interpret omnipresence as a licence for praying to and worshipping God wherever you are, there remains the paradox mentioned. Since earlier we laid some stress on the idea of a 'grammar' of gesture, it becomes puzzling if every bowing to God is also a bowing away. But let us stay with the conventions which control the language of gesture. Consider the situation in a typical Presbyterian building. There is no altar. It does not matter if the building does not face east. There are no images. A Martian anthropologist would perhaps initially be a bit puzzled. He would see people in the congregation, as they leave their pews, bowing in the direction of the top end of the building. He might conclude at first that there was something sacred about the communion table, or the vase of flowers placed on it. If he had previously done some field work among the Hindus he might even make the mistake of thinking that some god was specially present in the table or in the flowers or in both. What information would he get from asking the congregation? The trouble is that probably none of them will have thought about the question at all, and he would in fact get rather incoherent replies (even maybe angry ones, for it is very vexing, to say the least, when one discovers that one cannot quite account for an action which one has performed 'naturally' over the years, and which concerns what one regards as being a highly important aspect of one's life). But how would an answer be constructed? Would it not be something like the following? 'Of course God is everywhere, but he is specially present here in the church when we gather together. As Jesus said, When two or three are gathered together in my name. . . . So then God is specially with us. But we do not believe this in the way the Catholics do, when they as it were trap God in the consecrated host and put it in the tabernacle behind the altar, so that everyone coming into the church has to bend his knee before the God-thing. From our point of view that verges on the superstitious. For us God's presence is more spiritual and functional: he is with us in worship and in the preaching of the word. But you can't bow down before the preacher, for he is not God and is hopefully at best a vehicle only of God's power. So we bow towards the end of the church, not because we think of God as trapped in some thing up there. The beauty of it is that we have a place to bow to with nothing there to symbolise the Deity. In bowing that way we are bowing to a "place-holder", a conventional blank.'

35

This answer is doubtless too sophisticated for most of the pious, but it may help to bring out the spirit of symbolic directionality. But it may be noted that though the doctrine I have here ascribed to the Presbyterian worshipper is a good deal less given to concretisation than (say) traditional Catholicism, there is still a heavily symbolic element in it. If one took a very 'high' view of the doctrine of the Word as preached, then the central sacrament of the church is preaching (and hearing), and this is a shift of emphasis from the visible to the audible, and also from one sort of language to another. Why the shift? It is worth saying something briefly about this.

1.46. *Invisibility and blasphemy.* Is it just a coincidence that three, or rather two and a half, major religions have stressed that one should not make images of God? It could well be, for all stem in part at least from the same stock. It might be that the two and a half religions get the impression that idols are associated with polytheism. Since they stress very strongly the unity and indeed uniqueness of God, then they must be implacably opposed to anything which would stimulate poly-theism, even in that polite form which ultimately relates the many gods to the one Being (as often in Hinduism). We may note also that though there remain tendencies in the Bible (for example) to relate God more closely to some forces of nature rather than others – to thunder and the weather more than to the surging of the ocean or the waning of the moon – the main drive is towards freeing God from particular implication in nature. It is still true, as was pointed out earlier (1.43), that the cosmos remains in an important sense a particular – and of course God is also seen as acting in a particular way in the process of history; but nevertheless the cosmos is as it were emptied of its spirits and gods, to make way for the one great God who lies behind it, its Creator. (Actually, because of the need to assimilate other ideas and cults there is some truck with angels, who despite their godly appearance are firmly relegated to the role of messengers of God; while on the other hand there remains a certain messiness, notably in the New Testament, about evil forces – demons and the like. The drive to subsume them under one being, in this case Satan, is evident, but is less fervently insisted on than the comparable claims about the unity of God, perhaps for rather obvious reasons.) I am not entirely clear that a stress on the transcendence and uniqueness of God need entail anything about images, etc., but the argument for this position might go as follows. First, many actual gods are associated with forces of nature, and by the principle of likeness it becomes important to represent their likenesses. Thus images are bound up with natural particularities. Since God transcends these, he can best be symbolised by the absence of images. Second, since God is in some way personal, it follows that images of him will incorporate some resemblances to human beings (or lower, to animals). This brings the gods too much down to the human level and fails to signalise the otherness of God so importantly seen in the numinous experience. The more numinous a god, then, the less visible. But, it may be replied, surely the doctrine of the incarnation 'brings God down to the human level'. Does that make it blasphemous? The answer plainly is: Yes; prima facie it is blasphemous. This is the core of the offensiveness of the belief both to Jewish and Moslem sensibilities. In brief, there are ways of representing the invisibility of God, or rather of the absence of images of him, as being more than a mere contingency of the tradition of the Semitic religions. (There may, by the way, be other reasons for the lack of images: thus there was the mysterious absence of the Buddha figure in early Buddhist sculpture; his footprint might be there, a group of disciples and so on, but he was not there – a mysterious thing, but the probable explanation of it is that the blankness was a symbol of the fact that the Buddha could not be said to exist any more as an individual after his final decease, so that this blankness is not that of numinosity, of the unpicturability of the one supreme Being, but rather it is the blankness of the mystical cloud of unknowing, unbeing as it were. The two forms of blankness then have a very different significance – another warning that it is always very vital to contextualise in religion.)

1.47. *A note on superstition.* The suggestion was made by our putative Protestant exponent of why we bow down in the direction of the communion table, seeing that God is everywhere, that somehow the concretisation of God is blasphemous and superstitious. It is not our task here to determine what counts as superstition and what does not (it is very much the same question as that of the truth of a given religious system of belief and practice). There is too the old crack that one man's religion is another man's superstition: so often religious judgements are alas unkind. But apart from the argument advanced

37

in the previous paragraph, are there any reasons to think that concretisation (that is, the manifestation of God through images, sacraments and so on) tends more to a 'debased' religion than a more 'abstract' faith? The basis of the idea seems to lie in an ideology of a split between the spiritual and the material: where the spirit gets mixed up with matter then there is trouble. I leave it to the reader to ponder further developments of this theme, together with the problem of whether the ideology itself is justified.

1.48. *Invisibility and transcendence.* We have diverged a little from our path, so let us retrace our steps, and consider the problem of the invisibility of the gods as a sign of their transcending images, natural forces and other particularities. In regard to natural forces, part of the explanation lies in the very idea of a force being present here and there, wherever the force is manifested, for instance in fires, which body forth the god Agni. That there is one being present in many events suggests that the god both is and is not a given fire. It is instructive to consider how philosophers, taking over such a conception, entertained the possibility of universals, which, in the case of Plato's Forms, represent a similar notion to that of the gods. Though impersonal and so in this respect not like the gods, the universals strangely inhabit a superior realm (a notion which mirrors one way in which the gods' transcendence of the forces 'down here' is figured). Second, in regard to images, the god is, as we have seen in an earlier discussion, somewhat related to the image (within the frame) as a person is to his body. And just as it is not adequate to look on a person as a body, but rather as an entity that both involves and transcends a body, so too the god invisibly goes beyond his images. Combining these two accounts is natural enough also, for though it is right to think of the gods as personal (for they are addressed with words, etc.), it is not entirely wrong to treat them as substances or powers of which it is possible to partake (thus God is holy and something of his holiness is transferable). Gods float with ambiguity between the sharp features of the person and the undefined miasma of the magical substance.

1.49. *Transcendence and decks of the universe.* The gods go beyond their images and so forth, and one way this is expressed is by the belief in an upper deck of the universe (which is often three-decker, with us in between and the dark demonic realm below). The idea of an upper realm symbolically conveys the superiority of the gods, and so there is a match between the ritual and the ontology. But it would be a mistake to think that the literal idea of the upper world is a necessary way to convey the belief that God exists in a different and (so to say) higher place. We can recognise the symbolism of the heavenly without inconsistently swallowing it literally. I say 'inconsistently' because it has been known for a long time (much longer than the rise of modern science) that there is no heaven a short distance above the surface of the earth. And it has also been well known that alas astronomy and theology do not match. Or is it a matter of saying alas? For one of the lessons to learn about religion is that challenges to the mythic from the side of (say) science and rationalism can set in train a new process of understanding the hidden meanings of myths. However, be that as it may: the notion of transcendence can be explicated in terms of the non-spatiality of God and of his 'otherness' from the cosmos. One of the ways of repairing the effects of demythologisation – if indeed one wants to repair the damage – consists in the doctrinalisation of the previously mythically clothed message.

1.50. *Transcendence and omnipresence*. It would be a bit tedious to argue in detail what I have tried to set forth elsewhere, but the main sense that one can give to the thought that God has a place is in some sense 'beyond' the cosmos is that he exists, without spatial predicates attaching to him, in such a way that he is different from the cosmos and 'behind' it – that is, the force which makes and sustains it, so that from this point of view the doctrine of transcendence is strongly connected to the doctrine of creation. The idea, however, has a consequence, which is not immediately apparent. Since it involves treating 'behind' and 'beyond' as spatial analogies and so not as literal places, the *trans-* which introduces the concept of transcendence must suffer the same fate. Its Latin origin has no magical properties to defend it. Then one begins to ask a question or two about the supposedly contrasted idea of immanence. I realise that loosely the immanent refers to the particularities through which God manifests himself, while the transcendent represents the way in which God lies beyond these particularities. But leaving aside this so to say 'vulgar' contrast between the two ideas, and considering the other contrast sometimes attempted – where the

39

immanent refers to God's working in the world, e.g. through his preserving power, providentiality and so on – then one asks whether the distinction between this sense of the term and transcendence can be maintained. The reason is a simple one and can be put simply and crudely thus: When you say that God is in all things and when you say that God is beyond or behind all things, you appear to be saying two different things; but how can you be, considering that 'in', 'behind' and 'beyond' are analogical, not literal? And how can one aver that the differing analogical directions do not amount to the same direction? Literal space can be dealt with easily: if an ice-cream is in the fridge and not behind the fridge, then it is in one place and not in another and the in–behind contrast is applicable. But there can be no guarantee that this contrast can work when we come to analogical space. Thus there is no strong reason to differentiate between transcendence and immanence. Indeed there are some reasons of a doctrinal sort to encourage the identification of the two locations of God: for instance, because God's creative activity is not confined to his being there and the world not at the 'moment' of creation; but to the continuous creation of the world every day and every minute, working thus in all things. In brief there is no special reason to retain the old confused contrast. All of this of course relates to omnipresence. When we said earlier that the Creator is omnipresent, this amounted to saying that he is immanent everywhere. For inasmuch as God is a dynamic being his presence means work, and his being present everywhere thus means that he is working everywhere. It turns out then that when one begins to reflect doctrinally upon the location of God, the distinction between heaven and earth turns out to be drawn in a different place from that in which it had been imagined. It also turns out that the descriptions of God's power and sphere of activity becomes more abstract, less vivid and symbolic than in the mythic categories. This is doubtless a loss, and one would then need to ask if there are compensating gains. But to cut a long story short, it is unwise to look on the transcendence of God in terms of his being 'there' in heaven and manifesting himself down here upon earth. (This is not of course to deny that a certain mythic job may be done by such a description, in addition to making the point about the beyondness of God. There is a whole range of correspondences which are brought

40

out in mythic material, between the heavenly and the earthly realms and so forth, but that is another story.)

1.51. *A further summary on worship.* We can now add something to the summary given in 1.35. Beyond the four points mentioned, there lies a fifth: that the Focus of worship is transcendent, that it is not to be identified with the particularities (of whatever sort) through which he is manifested. We have tried to explain what transcendence and invisibility (in the relevant context) amount to. But there is a point about the holy and the unseen which the discussion so far has missed, and maybe it should now be introduced.

1.52. *The unseen and the covered gaze.* It is said that no man will see God and live. Whatever the correct interpretation is of that ancient text, it is a fairly widespread fact in the history of religions that closing the eyes, bowing the head (so that the gaze is downcast) and other means of screening the holy from profane gaze have been used. One of the troubles about the holy arises in the manner indicated earlier in our discussion of the rituals of superiority. The dynamics there adumbrated make contact with the holy dangerous; for the higher value of the holy wishes to deflect those who casually come into contact with it – contact being a primitive case of likeness (being in the same locale as the other at the same time, etc.). The likeness of the contacter to the holy could – to use quasi-electrical terms – cause a leak of holiness from the holy being to the contacter, unless counter-measures are brought into effect, such as symbolising the difference of the holy from any contacter. Similarly it is common to treat knowledge as a kind of contact, and one replete with power. The desire to retain the arcane is a sign of the dynamics of the holy and the desperate attempts made to keep the *status quo*. Since human beings know and come into contact initially most typically and splendidly through the use of vision, the eyes play a specially important part in the rituals of religion. It is not uncommon – as we have remarked above – for the eyes to be thought of as dangerous, for they bring immediate access to the object of perception and so diminish the power of the more powerful (the saying 'A cat can look at a king' is a remonstration against the eye-shielded humility of the liege). Thus it is not uncommon in religions for the holy of holies to be screened from profane gaze, and only opened up under carefully controlled conditions. Thus by extension it becomes possible to

41

look upon the world as a kind of screen, hiding God from our gaze, save when he 'breaks through' in a revelatory way. It is a dialectical situation: God hints at his glory through his handiwork, the world, but it also conceals him.

1.53. *Revelation and the veil.* Not at all unconnected with the foregoing is the very model built into the concept of revelation (apocalypse, etc.): namely that God is covered up, as it were by a veil, which is removed when he reveals himself. Sometimes this is figured as being dangerously numinous, as in the famous theophany of Krishna in the *Gita*, and as in a number of incidents in the Old Testament (consider Isaiah in the Temple). Thus the model is part of the use of the screen concept, and reinforces the invisibility of God. But, it will be answered, is there not an inconsistency here? For it is precisely in revelatory events that God is seen; and despite the saying that no man shall see God and live, people do see God and live. It is, however, necessary to distinguish; the seeing of God is not ordinary seeing, though it has an analogy to the latter. It has a visionary quality, as for Arjuna and Isaiah. It is thus even in the case of an incarnate God. Christ was as a man literally visible, but his divine outreach was not, save on revelatory occasions – for instance at the Transfiguration and the Resurrection, the accounts of both of which point to mysterious visionary aspects of the disciples' experience (I am not here concerned with the vexed question of the difficulty of knowing what to make of the historicity of these events and whether the Transfiguration is or is not a misplaced Resurrection narrative; we are here more concerned with the style of the concepts used than with their historical applicability).

1.54. *Revelatory occasions and grace.* It is likely that the screened character of God will be very sharply stressed in a monotheism, for it helps to take God right out of human reach, exalting beyond anything in the cosmos. The whole cosmos is his veil. The corresponding notion of revelation is also suggestive of the dynamic otherness of God, as though any contact with him, any knowledge of him, arises not by human action but by the spontaneous intervention of God himself. A sophisticated version of this sentiment is found in much modern evangelical theology, above all in that of Karl Barth. To some extent the debate about natural theology is about this and not about the validity of arguments that might be used to prove or make

42

probable God's existence. That is, the opponents of natural theology oppose it on theological rather than strictly philosophical grounds (nor is the trend confined to but one cultural tradition: one sees the same concern in Ramanuja, whose subtle arguments against the Argument from Design matched those of a much later Hume, but from a totally different perspective, to make way for grace rather than scepticism). So then, the idea of a spontaneous, gracious revelation is the epistemological cornerstone of the towering edifice of God's immeasurable superiority.

1.55. *Grace and the ritual of superiority.* The logic of the idea of grace can be spelled out in the following manner. The ritual of worship ascribes power to the Focus of worship. Suppose we consider that the Focus has unbounded power, how could one theorise about the ritual? The worshipper approaches the Focus and seems to come into contact. But any relevant goodness which he obtains from the Focus flows only in that direction. By contrast with the unbounded holiness of the Focus, the worshipper has no holiness. His obtaining any is in no way due to his own actions, even the ritual actions; but it is rather due to the action of the Focus. It is gracious action, because there can be no necessary ground for the merit that the worshipper gains from God. The ritual itself incorporates this complex of ideas into its substance, by repeating the words of contrition and unworthiness which are expressive of the hither side of the doctrine of grace, and by stressing the graciousness and mercy of the one Holy One. Thus an intense ritual directed at an unboundedly powerful and holy being will mesh with a doctrine of the spontaneous character of God's acts towards us. He is not constrained or obligated by what goes on down here. (All this cluster of ideas can then, in the Christian case, be applied to God's incarnation and sacrifice of himself upon the Cross.) However, it may be noted that the holy power may enter into some agreement; may bind himself voluntarily – as with the notion of the covenant in ancient Israel, and as too with the incarnations. Also the avatar, such as Krishna, does in some degree expose the god to risks. So much in general for the 'logic' of grace. Is what I have here propounded consistent, however, with what was stated earlier (1.35): namely that the ritual of worship sustains or forms part of the power of the Focus?

1.56. *Infinite holiness and earthly worship.* It should be made clear that the full doctrine of grace is found in the full monotheistic context, where God is worth infinite worship. The full doctrine does not apply in the case of lesser gods, which can up to a point be manipulated by human beings through the ritual (this is one way in which the exaltation of a single supreme Being moves religion along the spectrum away from sacred technology, or magic as it is sometimes called). But how is the full doctrine compatible with the theory that worship feeds the power and holiness of the supreme Being? If all holiness comes from God, how can man contribute? Is it not possibly a blasphemous conception? We run into a similar problem to that posed in the dialectic between grace (faith) and works. The solution is similar, not surprisingly. Thus in the one case good works are seen as symptomatic of true faith, and faith is seen as created by God himself. In the other case, the rite itself is divinely created in the first place and it is God's continued influence which brings it about that the cult is maintained.

1.57. *A further summary on worship*. We may now list fully the points being made about the nature of worship. First, it is a relational activity. Second, the ritual expresses the superiority of the Focus to the worshipper(s). Third, the ritual sustains or is part of the power of the Focus. Fourth, worship expresses the numinous experience and the Focus of worship is perceived as awe-inspiring. Fifth, the Focus of worship is unseen, i.e. transcends any particular manifestations of it that there may be. Sixth, the superiority of the Focus gives it greater power than the worshipper, and this gap is infinite in the case of an unboundedly supreme Being, so that the worshipper has no relevant merit, except in so far as this may be conferred on him by the supreme Being. We may now ask if the above account serves effectively to distinguish worship from activities, such as veneration of ancestors, saints, etc., and acting as a courtier, sycophant, etc., in relation to human beings. The investigation could become rather complex in view of the possibility of superimposition (1.4); and also in view of the fact that people may treat (say) other human beings as gods. However, we can at least sketch the differences between worship and these activities. We may note, incidentally, that in a given system of religious belief, the theology may state what entities are to be worshipped and what not, and this enters into the intentions of the adherents (consider how in Catholicism, that the *Ave Maria* sounds very much like worship – linguistically it is indistinguishable – nevertheless it is hedged with caveats about the role of the Virgin Mary, who is not of course divine).

1.58. *So-called ancestor worship.* In his book *African Religions and Philosophies* Joseph Mbiti sharply criticises the term 'ancestor worship'. He writes (p. 11):

> Certainly it cannot be denied that the departed occupy an important part in African religiosity; but it is wrong to interpret traditional religions simply in terms of 'worshipping the ancestors'. As we shall see later in this monograph, the departed, whether parents, brothers, sisters or children, form part of the family, and must therefore be kept in touch with their surviving relatives. Libation and the giving of food to the departed are tokens of fellowship, hospitality and respect; the drink and food so given are symbols of family continuity and contact. 'Worship' is the wrong word to apply in this situation: and Africans themselves know very well that they are not 'worshipping' the departed members of the family. It is almost blasphemous, therefore, to describe these acts of family relationships as 'worship'.

Why then was it easy for Westerners, following Herbert Spencer, to slip into thinking of the cult in this way (similarly with the cult of memorial tablets, etc., in traditional China)? The ancestor-cult fulfils very nearly the criteria we have listed above – with one major exception, however, and possibly two. First, the ancestors are not thought of as superior as such (of course an ancestor may be venerable and so superior to a child, say, who gives food and drink; but this would be just in the way in which a living venerable person is superior to a child). Second, ancestors are not specially numinous. This last remark may be challenged in view of the difficulty of distinguishing between the numinous and the uncanny (and surely the dead are uncanny). Do not the dead haunt us? And is not a ghost eminently awe-inspiring? (It was by making his tormentors sublimely oblivious of his awe-inspiring character that Oscar Wilde was able to depict the agonies of the unfortunate Canterville ghost.) But let us make various distinctions. Firstly, since living humans can be treated as gods, it is not here being denied that dead human beings may be so treated; but this is not the cult or the theology which is being discussed by Mbiti in referring to so-called ancestor worship. Second, many people

45

believe that if the dead are not looked after they will become hostile and dangerous. To discuss this aspect (which is highly relevant to the possible numinosity of ghosts), we need briefly to look at the nature of anti-gods.

1.59. *Gods and anti-gods.* Virtually throughout the discussion to date we have been assuming that worshippers approve of the beings they worship. Or rather, since 'approve' is a weak word, let us say that the gods are thought of as in principle benevolent, and the worshippers thus ally themselves to these beings. Of course some gods can be very fierce and not look at first sight as though they are very benevolent: Kali for instance, or Śiva in his more fearsome aspects. But we should not be carried away by external aestheticism, looking at these fierce gods as being somewhat malevolent because of their appearance to us. The worshipper of Kali does not consider Kali as evilly disposed towards him, in principle. Of course it may be that a worshipper has committed some sin against the god and awaits the god's wrath, but this is a conditional bad intent on the part of the god (and may be thought by the worshipper to be well justified). But though the gods are in principle good and beneficent to-wards the worshippers, there are other beings who are not, and who are indeed hostile. Consider Satan in Christianity and the lesser demons that plague us: Mara in the Buddhist tradition; the Asuras in the Veda; the Titans in ancient Greece. It is not especially our business here to inquire into how the anti-gods arise (sometimes they are the gods of a hostile group; one man's anti-god is another man's god, and conversely). Now one would not wish to speak of worshipping an anti-god; one does not worship anti-gods. Or does one? Consider the strange business of worshipping the Devil.

1.60. *On worshipping the Devil.* Satanism, obviously enough, takes various forms. Let us begin with a simple version. A person is accused of worshipping the Devil. She identifies the Devil with the god of her ancestors. Thus though it is in a sense true that she worships the Devil, this is an exterior description, from outside her frame (1.13). It would best be put like this: She worships X, which her accusers identify with the Devil that they repudiate. This example causes, then, no problem, and does not offend against the rule that one does not worship what one counts as an anti-god. Another case is where the question of the status of the Devil, whether as on our side or against us, is scarcely raised: here again the general principle would not be infringed. The trickiest case is where the cultist cries, in the style of Iago: 'Evil, be thou my good.' It is indeed a deep question to understand fully the meaning of this cry. But it might at least involve allying himself with an evil Force (the Devil), knowing it to be evil, because of his hatred of good people: their destruction thus is good for him and the agent of destruction, the Devil, then in a sense is beneficent, without, however, the benefit of morality. Thus it still remains true that one does not worship anti-gods: the Devil as god is merely a highly sectarian choice, in which the evil rebel sets himself against society at large.

1.61. *Apotropaic rites and the anti-gods.* Though a god may threaten us, for we may have done some sin against him, in general a god can be relied on to be some sort of ally. But what of an anti-god? Such a being can be relied on generally to be hostile. It is thus his 'function' to do us down. How do we reinforce the beneficent power of the god? By feeding his power with the rituals of worship (sacrifice, etc.). It would seem to follow that there must be an 'anti-rite' to deal with the anti-gods. This is not a ritual of worship; it does not bless or magnify – rather it curses and minimises. Sometimes such rites may be modified by the knowledge that the anti-gods are powerful, so it may be wise to be careful. Just as one shares in the holiness and good of the good god, so one must turn away the evil power of the evil one. But a rite of turning away cannot properly be described as an act of *worship*, unless of course the cultists invoke the good god to turn away the evil spirit.

1.62. *Ghosts again.* So when the dead turn nasty and haunt us, we may use various apotropaic rites; but these do not count as worship. Why, incidentally, do they turn nasty in this way? Since the rite of passage for the dead is undertaken by the family, it is they who will attract attention if the rite is not properly performed. The rite puts the dead to rest; and restless dead folk can only badger those who have the secret of their being put to rest. Hence too the idea that exceptionally evil people after they die continue to haunt us: they cut themselves off from their society in this life, and thus have no one to put them to rest. To sum up about ancestors: the marks of worship sufficiently account for the fact that ancestor-cults are not in the proper sense worship.

1.63. *Worship and the veneration of saints*. History shows us ways in which some cults of saints are built on the earlier basis of pagan cults. This is notable in some Mediterranean countries and in Mexico and other parts of Latin America. But it does not follow from this that such 'venerations' of saints should be counted as worship. As has been suggested before, it partly turns on the intentions of the participants in these cults. And it will be a delicate matter to disentangle these with accuracy. Disentangle? Here comes the question: What *is* the supposed difference between worship and veneration, so that one could differentiate attitudes and intentions? Saints are holy, superior to the cultist, numinous in their miracle-working, invisible – transcending their plaster statues. They seem thus to have the marks of gods. On the other hand, it would be blasphemous (in the Christian context) to treat them as gods or to suggest that they are to be worshipped, for there is but one God, and all worship must be directed at him. Is such adherence to the doctrine of monotheism mere inconsistency, or worse, hypocrisy? Some Protestants have thought of the Catholic saints as if they were gods and so blasphemous and a betrayal of Christianity.

1.64. *A theory of saints*. Let us note that saints have to exist as human beings. Saints whose existence becomes doubtful get struck off the list, like poor St George. They also have to belong to the Christian tradition (it is rather embarrassing that the story of St Josaphat turns out to be referring to the Bodhisattva – the Buddha before his enlightenment, giving up the world, the flesh and the devil in a good medieval manner). Now according to the theory of saints, their sanctity is based upon their deeds in this life: the matter of miracle-working is more a criterion to be used to diagnose sainthood, and so can be brought about after the saint's death. But their good actions in this life are ultimately due to God. It is God who sanctifies. Thus the holiness possessed by the holy man is derivative, according to the theory. Thus one can as it were worship God by reference to the saints, for they reflect God's holiness. The situation could be described in a 'material' way as follows. Imagine holiness to be a substance, centrally possessed and generated by God. God can detach bits of the substance and attach it to other beings, such as angels and saints (and even consecrated things). The beings begin to take on a divine aspect; but cannot be considered, according to orthodox doctrine, as being independent gods, for

48

the holiness they possess is not intrinsic to them. It is at this point that historical observations may turn out to be rather important, for if a given saint is the historical successor of a god, to whom numinosity *did* intrinsically belong, it becomes less easy to maintain the orthodox account. This is one way in which one would approach the problem of disentangling veneration from worship.

1.65. *Worship and being a courtier*. It could similarly be thought that in some circumstances the ritual court behaviour becomes so close to being worship as to be indistinguishable from it. Consider too the veneration of the monk's robe in Buddhism. First, though, it is necessary to make a distinction. Clearly, almost anything can be deemed a god in some culture or other, and we do not have to look far into the history of the ancient Near East to discover divine kingship. That a king is a living god is a natural enough arrangement in certain cultural–political situations. So in such a case the courtiers are not mere courtiers: they actually do worship the king – just as they may also worship the sun. But what about the Sun King? Or the splendid Defender of the Faith? How does one distinguish the deference ritually shown to them from worship proper? Again we have to look to intentions. The Sun King does not have 'behind' him the invisible outreach of the god; nor probably does he have the full flavour of numinosity, though he may well be fear-inspiring and awe-inspiring. Thus though praise ('Hail Caesar'), prayers ('Sire, hear my petition') and ritual acts of bowing down occur, matching what may go on in worship proper, the king is still not conceived as a holy god. It is interesting in the Christian context how the divine ambience of kingship is treated derivatively, like the holy ambience of the saint. The king may have divine right: he may cure the 'king's disease', he may defend the faith – but these properties are conferred on him (according to the theory) by God and are not intrinsic to him. A similar tactic is employed to give a clear indication of the difference between the king, however exalted he may be in this transitory world, and God; and thus between obsequiousness of lieges and worship proper. (Lord mayors in England, incidentally, being lesser folk and so in need of greater effort to bolster their mini-exaltation, are given the title that was taken over for religion – 'Your worship'.)

1.66. *Worship and prayer*. It is hard to see that there can be a

49

prayer which does not involve worship; but there are forms of prayer which are not necessary to worship, such as petition, for one can worship God without petitioning him. This introduces a point about worship which we have not hitherto made: about the expansibility of what counts as an act of worship. For instance, if I mutter under my breath 'Praise be to thee, O Lord', this is an act of worship, but a very brief, and incidentally 'pure', one – 'pure' because it is simply a bit of praising and nothing else. On the other hand, we might consider a whole religious service as being an act of worship – indeed the name for the main service in many free churches is 'Divine Worship', corresponding to Mass, say, in the Catholic tradition. It is a whole sequence of individual events woven together into a coherent whole. The expanded act of worship – the whole service – may well include a number of activities which are not in the strict sense worship. Thus a reading from the Gospel, though done for the greater glory of God, is not primarily an act of worship; nor is the preaching of a sermon; nor giving one another the kiss of peace; nor for that matter is receiving communion. But note how these activities tend to be prefaced with praise within the service, to signalise their being part of an extended intention to worship. Thus a Gospel reading can be prefaced with 'Praise be to thee O Lord'.

1.67. *Worship and praise*. It has been implied in the foregoing that praise is somehow an integral part of the act of worship. It is now time for us to approach the question of the overlap between these two important concepts. This will enable us, moreover, to conclude this first part, which aims to have given a general characterisation and placement of the concept of worship. There are certainly differences between worship and praise. But what are they? First, you can praise a person to a third party, not directly to his face. But worship cannot thus be indirectly conducted. (Though other uses of religious language can in this way be third-person, and such uses may be woven into an extended act of worship: for instance 'May the Lord in his infinite mercy have pity on your soul'.) In worshipping God one addresses him, but one does not need to address him to praise him. Second, praise can be 'secular', and so one can praise a child for his cleverness or good conduct, or praise a famous cricketer for his deeds. But it is only in a secondary metaphorical sense that one can worship something 'secular'

50

(like one's stomach, as we saw earlier). Third, one of superior status can praise someone of inferior status, but this is not so with worship. Fourth, there is a linguistic asymmetry: 'What are you praising him for?' is natural enough, but 'What are you worshipping him for?' has rather a different kind of meaning. This can be brought out thus. To praise a child for tidying his room involves specifying that in the praise, and one can still go on to ask the question 'What are you praising that child for tidying up his room for?' The right answer begins 'Because . . .'; just as the answer to 'What are you worshipping God for?' starts in the same way. So much then for certain differences in the manner in which the two concepts are used. How do they overlap? Is praise a necessary feature of worship? That is, could one worship without praising? I think not. It is true that if one uttered a silent prayer as a form of worship one would not be overtly praising, but this would have to be understood by reference to the overt case – for praising involves the use of language. But of course the 'style' of praise will be different in the worshipping context from that of the praise used in secular contexts, in accordance with the various characteristics of worship.

1.68. *Summing up and the general account of worship.* We have left unresolved a problem (1.10) about the possibility of identifying different – or supposedly different – gods. This we shall come back to in the next part, which takes up a number of philosophical problems to which the general account of worship is relevant. But we have argued that: worship is relational; it typically involves ritual; this ritual expresses the superiority of the Focus; it also sustains or is part of the power of the Focus; the experience which worship tries to express is the numinous, and the object of worship is thus perceived as awe-inspiring; worship involves praise, but addressed direct to the Focus; this Focus transcends, however, the manifestations. All this implies the personalised character of the Focus. Though we have not argued the point separately, it becomes evident that the foci of worship, God or the gods, need to be understood in the context provided by worship. That is, there is an internal relationship between the concepts of god and of worship. Thus we might seem to accept that naïve and simplistic analytic truth: that a god is to be worshipped (analytic since a god is defined as a being who is to be worshipped) – but the utterance does suffer

51

some sea change at the end of an exploration, for it is in the light of the whole context of ritual, numinosity, etc., that one can come to see that a god is to be worshipped, though in giving the account of worship one has to draw out the ways in which the foci function, as gods.

1.69. *The propriety of worshipping a god.* But it will be objected that we often come across, in the history of religions, denials that a particular god is to be worshipped. Baal, for instance. But a god one should not worship shifts over to become either a thing of nought or an anti-god. Or at least this roughly is true: one can have subtle variegations – thus it might be held by one group that it was not its job to worship god A, but rather this was the job of group B. But this would still be a system where the god was recognised as to be worshipped, though there would be division of labour, so to say.

PART TWO

God's Existence

2.1. *Worship and the alleged disproof of God's existence.* An argument which has attempted in a sense to use phenomenology is J. N. Findlay's celebrated 'Can God's Existence be Disproved?' His position has changed somewhat since he wrote that article, but it is useful to look at the points made by him at that time. The core of the argument is that only a necessary being is really fit to be worshipped: but the notion of necessary being is incoherent; thus the true God cannot exist. Findlay, however, adds, with characteristic subtlety, that you can have as profound a reverence for a *focus imaginarius* as for a real being (there is almost a Buddhist flavour to his thinking here, as though his God could be Void, a non-thing). However, the nerve of the argument turns on the question of what is worthy to be worshipped. I do not here wish to consider the question of necessary being – I shall accept Findlay's point here and the general criticisms of the Ontological Argument in recent philosophical literature.

2.2. *Is a merely contingent God worthy to be worshipped?* It is notable that Findlay, like many others, starts with a very high conception of God: he must be utterly exalted; that than which no lesser can be worshipped, as one might put it. Let us accept this conception for the sake of argument, but let us note in passing that it puts out of court many of the lesser rites of men and might perhaps be unjust to them (classifying them as superstitious, but as we have already asked: What are the criteria?). The question is: What if God is contingent? Does this make him unworthy of worship? Let us look now in detail to what Findlay says (*Mind*, n.s. LVII 179):

But now we advance further – in company with a large number of theologians and philosophers, who have added new touches to the portrait of deity, pleading various theoretical necessities, but really concerned to make their

55

object worthier of our worship – and ask whether it isn't wholly anomalous to worship anything *limited* in any thinkable manner. For all limited superiorities are tainted with an obvious relativity, and can be dwarfed in thought by still mightier superiorities, in which process of being dwarfed they lose their claim upon our worshipful attitudes. And hence we are led on irresistibly to demand that our religious object should have an *unsurpassable* supremacy along all avenues, that it should tower *infinitely* above all other objects. . . . But we are also led on irresistibly to a yet more stringent demand, which raises difficulties which makes the difficulties we have mentioned seem wholly inconsiderable: we can't help feeling that the worthy object of our worship can never be a thing which merely *happens* to exist, nor one on which all other objects merely *happen* to depend.

2.3. *Problems in Findlay's argument.* Findlay holds that worship is a ritual expressing the superiority of its Focus, much in the way in which this has been outlined. But he wants to insist on the *infinite* superiority of God, and in this he has good warrant from the Judaeo–Christian and other traditions. But there is some difficulty as to what this *infinity* amounts to. To this we shall return. Let us first consider what can be meant, on Findlay's account, by necessity and contingency. Since he is using the 'modern' view that existence cannot be necessary which is a view about what can and what cannot count as necessary truths, he must essentially mean that God's existence is not *logically* contingent: that is, that 'God does not exist' is, for the worshipper, inconceivable. First, is it true of worshippers? It may turn out that there are saintly worshippers who if they were asked whether it is a self-contradiction to suppose that God did not exist would deny that this was so. But even if we found such people, Findlay could still argue that their theology was somehow inferior – they ought not to be thinking in this way. But why not? Is a necessary being *superior* to a contingent one? It seems very odd to suppose that because of a distinction (on the modern view) between different types of statements one can make value-judgements about what they are about. There is a suggestion in Findlay's argument that he is sliding from one sense of contingent to another – it might superficially be supposed that because X depends on Y for its existence, then X is inferior to Y (even this is highly doubtful, as we shall see); but this is not the same sense as logical contingency – and it does not follow that because something is referred to in a logically contingent statement it is dependent on something else for its existence. Thus 'The speed of light is such-and-such' is contingent, but it is hard to know what it means to say that light is dependent on something else for its existence. In any case, if it were thought that independence was the prized characteristic of God – i.e. his not being contingent, in the non-logical sense, on other beings – this could (so to say) be arranged. That everything else depends on God would follow indeed from the doctrine of creation. But this concept – of a being on whom all others depend – is not equivalent to the notion of a necessary being.

2.4. *Logical contingency and what happens to be.* Nor does it follow, if God is considered not to be necessary (in the logical sense – though strictly here we speak uncouthly, having dropped from the proper level for the application of logical necessity and contingency, namely the level of statements), that he just *happens* to exist, as Findlay suggests. For happenings are related to human purposes, wishes and so on. Thus 'When I was attacked, I grabbed a stick that happened to be lying on the table'; that is, it came in convenient, though I did not cause it to be there – an accident fitting in with a purpose. Again: 'I saw something horrible happen on the motorway: a lorry jack-knifed and two cars ran into it'; that is, an accident contrary to human purposes. Still, some uses of 'happen' bring it close to the notion of coincidence. Some things cannot be explained, though this is not to say that anything random has occurred – for example, Bury, Blackpool and Burnley may lose next Saturday. If they do it is merely a coincidence that they all begin with B. 'It so happened,' we might say, 'that all the clubs beginning with B lost.' But it does not follow that because something cannot be explained it is a coincidence. In what sense then is it supposed that if God exists he merely *happens* to do so? Consider: suppose we say that there is no Creator, so that we simply have to take the existence of the cosmos as a brute fact. It then is logically contingent (for we do not wish to describe the cosmos as a necessary being, presumably); but in what sense do we say that the cosmos merely *happens* to exist? We are surely way beyond the realm of coincidences. Besides, what is wrong

57

with merely happening to exist? Suppose a couple have a child by mistake: they do not plan or wish to have one, but it so happened that they miscalculated seasons or did not notice a defect in the contraceptive. The child born merely happens, it could be said, to exist – but he might be a Beethoven or a saint. Does his value diminish because of his accidentality? (Well, he might worry if he got to know of it, as to whether his parents really love him as much as his sibling who was 'planned', but this does not affect his intrinsic value – a person can be of high value but cost money, etc.)

2.5. *Contingency and the infinite.* The suggestion of Findlay's argument is that an infinite being cannot be logically contingent. But what is an infinite being? In this content, that of worship, an infinite being is one of unbounded worship-value. To call God infinitely great is similar to saying that he is unspeakably great; here we revert to the analysis given earlier (1.37). Note too that 'great' here is pretty much a place-filling word, an expressive blank (as in 'It was a great meal' – this does not mean that there was much of it, I presume: asparagus and broiled lobster makes a great meal, greater than porridge and spaghetti). This point will also be relevant to our discussion of Malcolm's resurrection of the Ontological Argument, which has another sort of appeal to greatness. It would seem to me that God could be unspeakably good to us (for instance) though he might not have been, e.g. by sending his Son to save us, so that his 'infinite' goodness would rest upon a contingency. (Incidentally it is probably correct to reject the assumption made by C. B. Martin in *Religious Belief* and in his article 'The Perfect Good' that God is necessarily good; the point being that it was something of a 'discovery' in the history of, say, the Judaeo–Christian tradition – that is, numinosity and goodness do not entail one another; it is thus more like a theoretical than a logical necessity that God is good, it being a proposition heavily entrenched in the system and now highly central to it.)

2.6. *Contingency and perfections.* Is there something imperfect about not being a logically necessary being? There are problems in disentangling different notions of perfection, but let us try, a little briefly and crudely. First, a thing can be perfect in the sense that it is a flawless specimen of a species, like a diamond. Second, a thing can be perfect in that it is very, very good and any subtraction or addition might spoil it – as when one might

58

say that *The Marriage of Figaro* is a perfect opera, or that 'we spent a perfect evening together'. In neither of these two senses are perfections jealous of one another – thus the fact that one opera is perfect does not prevent another one also from being so; and the fact that one diamond is perfect does not prevent another one from being so. Thus it is so far a fallacy to suppose that things are arranged on a scale of goodness such that there is at the top a single perfect thing. Nor does a thing's being perfect prevent it from being contingent – even in the non-logical sense. Why then should necessary existence be a perfection? A brief comment on one aspect of Anselm is useful.

2.7. *In reality and in the intellect.* It is true that we can sometimes frame ideas of perfections that have never been realised – e.g. perhaps no skater has yet performed a perfect figure of eight (specified within an accuracy of a certain sort), so that it might be argued in the style of Anselm somewhat that at present we have instances of pretty good figures of eight, together with the unrealised idea of the perfect performance. There is a sense in which it is better for the performance to exist out there than merely in my mind. But it is not a more perfect something than the idea in my mind. So if we are to work an Ontological Argument we need to shift from perfection to the notion of being better or worse. But a better *what?* Is a God who exists a better God than a God who does not exist? And in any event, can we not turn round Findlay's argument? You might think that the most excellent being must exist necessarily (in the logical sense), but such an idea is self-contradictory, so the most excellent being, you might have thought, cannot exist. Yes, except that I prefer my beings not to be self-contradictory, so I prefer to worship the most perfect being thinkable, that is one with all sorts of excellences and no self-contradictions – that is an excellently contingent being!

2.8. *Malcolm's variant.* In his well-known article 'Anselm's Ontological Arguments' Norman Malcolm argues in the opposite direction to Findlay, but nevertheless explicates the idea of an infinite being in a way that has analogies to the treatment afforded by Findlay. To this I shall turn in a moment; but first let us note what Malcolm says about necessary being:

The correct reply [sc. to Findlay's argument] is that the view that logical necessity merely reflects the use of words cannot possibly have the implication that every existential proposition must be contingent. That view requires us to *look at* the use of words and not manufacture *a priori* theses about it. In the Ninetieth Psalm it is said: 'Before the mountains were brought forth, or ever thou hadst formed the earth and the world, even from everlasting to everlasting thou art God.' Here is expressed the idea of the necessary existence and eternity of God, an idea that is essential to the Jewish and Christian religions. In those complex systems of thought, those 'language-games', God has the status of a necessary being. Who can doubt that? Here we must say with Wittgenstein, 'This language-game is played!'

There are numerous troubles in this exposition. First, is a religion a language-game or is religion? If the former, then perhaps we can say that God is necessary to a given game; but then one does not need to play the game, so there is another way, from an external perspective in which it is possible to say 'There is no God' (unless you have to be playing the game to understand it; but what of someone who ceases to play? Does he suddenly forget his understanding of it? – this is a difficulty with the whole position outlined in D. Z. Phillips's challenging *The Concept of Prayer*.) Second, it is not at all clear that the Ninetieth Psalm is saying that God is a necessary being, or implying it. On the surface it seems to be saying that God is everlasting, while Malcolm interprets this as meaning also that God is eternal (which could be a different concept, timelessness and everlastingness being different). To say that God is everlasting is not to say that he is necessary. The cosmos, for instance, may be everlasting (it would be presumably if the steady-state cosmology were right, and would be also if the pulsating model were accepted), but this does not mean that it is necessary. If it did, by the way, Malcolm might find himself in a Spinozistic frame of mind. Something that had no beginning might not have existed (from the point of view of our applying logical contingency). In brief, Malcolm's account here is somewhat dubious, and it is not clear that he has shown that the notion of necessary being has a necessary place in religious discourse – it could be a philosophical importation.

2.9. *Malcolm and guilt.* Another aspect of Malcolm's argument is worth consideration, as it bears more directly on the practice of worship. He writes (p. 60):

> But even if one allows that Anselm's phrase may be free of self-contradiction, one wants to know how it can have any *meaning* for anyone. Why is it that human beings have even *formed* the concept of an infinite being, a being greater than which cannot be conceived? This is a legitimate and important question. I am sure there cannot be a deep understanding of that concept without an understanding of the phenomena of human life that give rise to it. To give an account of the latter is beyond my ability. I wish, however, to make one suggestion (which should not be understood as autobiographical).

We shall see what that suggestion is in a moment. Meanwhile, I would agree strongly that Malcolm is right to look at the non-linguistic context to shed light on the provenance of the Anselmian notion (which as we have seen he detects more widely in the ancient Judaic tradition). It is, by the way, interesting that Europe is the only civilisation to have produced the Ontological Argument, though what this portends is obscure. From Malcolm's point of view, India abounds with necessary beings – selves for instance are eternal. But let us proceed to his suggestion. He writes (p. 60):

> There is the phenomenon of feeling guilt for something that one has done or thought or felt or for a disposition that one has. One wants to be free of this guilt. But sometimes the guilt is felt to be so great that one is sure that nothing one could do oneself, nor any forgiveness by another human being, would remove it. One feels a guilt that is beyond all measure, a guilt 'a greater than which cannot be conceived'.... Out of such a storm in the soul, I am suggesting, there arises the conception of a forgiving mercy that is limitless, beyond all measure. ... I wish only to say that there *is* that human phenomenon of an unbearably heavy conscience and that it is importantly connected with the genesis of the concept of God, that is, with the formation of the 'grammar' of the word 'God'.

Malcolm is here seeming to make an empirical hypothesis. It would take a long time to establish whether it were true; all that

61

I can offer are some observations which tend to show that it is not true.

2.10. *Against Malcolm and guilt.* First, we must note that the concept of guilt is in part at least an ethical one. It is doubtful whether the idea of an infinite necessary being is intrinsically related to guilt. For instance, on Malcolm's account necessity has to do with eternity. But what has this to do with guilt? I would have thought that eternity has more to do with hope than with despair. Second, guilt concerns moral action; and though it is correct to see that moral actions can be seen as being offences (for example) against the Lord, this does not at all entail that they must be given a religious interpretation. Malcolm gives backing to his position with a quotation from Kierkegaard (*The Journals*, ed. A. Dru, sc. 936): 'There is only one proof of the truth of Christianity and that, quite rightly, is from the emotions, when the dread of sin and a heavy conscience torture a man into crossing the narrow line between despair bordering upon madness – and Christianity.' But there are questions about this too. Is Kierkegaard putting the emotional cart before the ritual horse? For it might be argued as follows: the concept of sin has its origin and placement in man's confrontation with the Holy, in worship and in the numinous experience. It then becomes applied more widely to the sphere of moral action. Perhaps guilt is intelligible independently of the concept of the divine, but sin is not (so much so that in these latter, rather godless days, sin simply becomes a synonym for the morally wrong, with special reference often, interestingly enough, to sexual misdemeanours, as in the title of a naughty film *House of Sin*). Thus Kierkegaard is wrong in suggesting that one can have a dread of sin which is not already specifically linked to awe of holiness. Further, even given the premiss that there is only one proof of Christianity, namely from the emotions, it in no way follows that these have to be 'negative' rather than 'positive' ones (dread of sin rather than joy at holiness).

2.11. *Proof and conversion.* It might be thought that my criticism of Kierkegaard gets me into a circularity: for if, to know that God exists, it is necessary to experience sentiments conveyed through worship, then one cannot know that God exists without worshipping him. But worshipping him presupposes belief that he does. The circle, however, is scarcely a vicious one – for one might come to believe in Christianity without having 'proof' or rather existential conviction of its truth. Further, it is possible for people to experience the sentiments as 'participant observers' rather than as believers. This in fact seems to be what happens quite frequently when conversions occur. Also, though it may be that to 'know' that God exists one must experience him numinously, and so in the general context of ritual, some of the spirit of such knowledge can be conveyed outside that context. Rudolf Otto for example was over-modest in supposing that those who had not had the numinous experience could not understand his famous book; for he succeeds very well in conveying the spirit of the numinous.

2.12. *Kierkegaard again.* Though I have here criticised the position expressed by Kierkegaard and endorsed by Malcolm, it does not mean that I consider Kierkegaard's 'analysis' to be irrelevant. His anatomy of the emotions, such as dread, indicates a territory where there is as it were some congruence with what is experienced in the rituals of worship. Thus there can be a 'superimposition' of the concepts of worship upon psychology, just as there can be superimposition of them upon moral action. That there must be some congruence is brought out in the moral case by seeing that certain attitudes and acts are more naturally interpreted in this way than others – humility as humility before God, giving things up for other people as a form of sacrifice, and so on. Dread matches the 'fear of the Lord' experienced in the numinous; serene calm matches eternal unchangeability, etc. However, it becomes misleading to detach these sentiments from active relationship to God, as though one could – so to say – abolish the religious milieu that give them divine significance while retaining the essence of the faith.

2.13. *Worship and the 'Protestant' principle.* Yet it may be protested that Kierkegaard is only doing what is in accord with Protestant principles, namely interiorising the cult – stressing the attitudes rather than the outer actions. Certainly one would not want to defend hypocritical and superficial religion, which simply contents itself with going through the outer actions. Nor do we want to adopt a wrong sort of ritualism, it will be said. The way to do this is to remember that it is the inner faith of the individual which counts in the last resort. However, though faith is clearly important, it is difficult to believe that a satisfactory definition of God by reference to psychological attitudes will turn out to be satisfactory. Consider one conclusion that this path may lead to.

2.14. *Cantwell Smith and the meaning and end of religion*. Wilfred Cantwell Smith has written a very challenging and important book, and though I consider that its conclusions are open to severe criticism, this does not minimise the significance of Smith's work. In many ways his strictures upon the modern idea of 'religions' as separate systems is enlightening. Two features of his thinking make it convenient to contemplate his position. One is that he exhibits the 'Protestant principle' which I referred to in the previous paragraph; second, he also posits a single end or focus of religion, namely God, and this raises questions about how one can tell whether the adherents of two faiths are after all worshipping the same God. Some consideration of this topic will bring us back to issues dealt with near the beginning of this essay.

2.15. *Faith and relationship to God*. Cantwell Smith writes (p. 191):

> My faith is an act that *I* make, naked before God. Just as there is no such thing as Christianity (or Islam or Buddhism), I have urged, behind which the Christian (the Muslim, the Buddhist) may shelter, which he may set between himself and the terror and splendour and living concern of God, so there is no generic Christian faith; no 'Buddhist faith', no 'Hindu faith', no 'Jewish faith'. There is only my faith, and yours, and that of my Shinto friend, of my particular Jewish neighbour. We are all persons, clustered in mundane communities no doubt, and labelled with mundane labels but, so far as transcendence is concerned, encountering it each directly, personally, if at all. In the eyes of God each of us is a person, not a type.

A number of propositions can be elicited from this paragraph: first, that each faith is particular; second, that religions are both reifications and means of escape from the confrontation with God; third, that each person in the differing traditions is faced by the transcendent (also referred to as God). There is some shifting of Cantwell Smith's position in the book as to whether the transcendent is the same for every man (see what he says on p. 186, for instance), but there is little doubt that this is his

64

belief. There is also little doubt that he prefers the term 'God' for it. Thus he writes (p. 305):

> For convenience in simplifying the argument, we speak here of God. . . . The substance of our argument is not significantly modified by any modification in terminology here that might be useful for greater exactitude: not even in the case of those less sophisticated traditions where the transcendent element in the community's life may not be conceptualised denominatively at all. To phrase the point with perhaps more clarity and acceptability, but no more precision: the participant is concerned with what I, a Christian, term God.

There are, of course, notorious difficulties in trying like this to speak of a single something which is the Focus of different men's faith, as Cantwell Smith himself agrees. Thus it is to say the very least rather doubtful whether one can properly see the main Focus of the Buddhism of the Theravada or of the Śūnyavāda (Voidist) school as at all like God, for reasons which have been partly sketched earlier in the discussion of the difference between worship and contemplation. But let us leave aside this particular difficulty, and stay with people who have faith in such Beings as God (Christ), Allah, Viṣṇu, Yahweh. Here one can certainly make out a case for treating these Foci all as transcendent in an appropriate sense of the term. But what of its flavour? Can one adequately define it in terms of the faith-relationship? Now obviously Cantwell Smith is not affirming that every person's faith is the same (and he rightly talks about faith varying from one day to another in the case of the individual). A person's faith results in part at least from the cumulative tradition which he inherits; or rather it is *shaped* by this. Its shape is as it were the product of the interplay between the transcendent and the cultural heritage of the person. Thus Cantwell Smith is not saying that there is a single faith which is somehow definitory of the nature of the transcendent. But he is on the other hand, I think, claiming that one can understand the nature of the transcendent through encounters, that is through the experiences of the faithful, and there is more than a hint that that experience has common elements, however diffracted the supernal light may be by the glass through which it is seen so dimly, so often, and so variously. This is implicit in

65

the earlier passage which I quoted (referring to the terror, splendour and loving concern of the transcendent). It is encountering *this* which engenders true faith. Conversely if one asks what the nature of God truly is, one does not turn to the various doctrines and myths which have been used to express men's various styles of faith, but rather to the vivid experience which the practice of religion can bring. Since people's response to the transcendent can vary, one can speak of people's being more or less religious or indeed of my being more religious yesterday than today – and much of this, as Cantwell Smith says elsewhere, has to do with character. (Faith shines through a man's character: Cantwell Smith is not thinking of the stiff-upper-lip sense of the term.) But at heart it is by pointing to experience that one knows the nature of God. In brief: God is experientially defined.

2.16. *A critique of the 'Protestant principle' but not of Protestantism.* The thesis which Cantwell Smith is putting forward runs somewhat contrary to the position which I have here maintained, in that I have stressed the place of ritual, the relatively public nature of concepts of the Focus of worship and the need to see God as a concept formed in the milieu of worship. There seem to be some objections to Smith's position. First, it is not altogether clear what religion is, that is, what the nature is of that which we may use to shield ourselves from God (here of course Cantwell Smith is to some degree influenced by the writings of Karl Barth and by the latter's contrast between the Gospel and religion). But in so far as it involves the rituals of worship, then Cantwell Smith seems to be saying that these can be a shield. Well, in one way they can be. For the pious person may see that it is the right response to God to fall on one's knees in adoration of him – this is the appropriate reaction to the terror and splendour and loving concern about which Cantwell Smith wrote in one of the passages which I have quoted. But the pious person, while recognising that kneeling is the right thing to do, may not after all be very sincere; or more likely he may be afraid that if he takes the terror too seriously his life may become disturbed too much. If what folk say about God is true, then he might be a hard taskmaster. So it comes about that the pious person knows what to do, but does it gingerly, just to satisfy proprieties. Who would not worship the creator of the cosmos? So I worship him. But this does not mean that I change my life. In such circumstances one can see how it is that the adherence to formal piety does constitute a kind of shield against the terror and the splendour. Religion in this sense can certainly be used. But it does not follow that there cannot be someone else who is not afraid of the terror and the splendour and who equally knows that the right response is to fall on his knees in adoration of the Holy One, and who worships him in all sincerity, and applies his vision to his daily life, in loving concern for others. But the two people whose attitudes I have here sketched are actually doing the same thing, though the one's intentions are different from the other's – and what it is that they are doing is worshipping God. Is it not then rather confusing to bracket both these activities together as constituting that 'religion' which has to be transcended? What more can the second person do? He has transcended the outer show already. What more is there then to do? Throw away worship? But that is to deprive the second man not only of the means by which he expresses his faith in the overpowering otherness of the God whom he addresses, but also makes a difference to the very concept of God.

2.17. *A diversion on the concept of religion.* It was never the intention of Bonhoeffer to ban prayer; his was a secret and yet also public faith, in the style of Hamann. His notion of a 'religionless Christianity' did, however, carry over something from the position of Barth (and others – for instance Brunner and Kraemer, whose *The Christian Message in a Non-Christian World* exploited rather heavily the rift between the Gospel on the one hand and man's religion, including the Christian religion, on the other). The main nisus therefore of those who are critical of 'religion' in some special sense needs to be taken seriously. Yet there is a practical paradox; for those who preach the rift are typically very faithful in their observances of worship, prayer and church attendance – for they are theologians, after all, and thus are spokesmen and adherents of the Christian tradition. From one point of view the distinction is a means of prophesying, that is of criticising the current order in the Church. The strictures on religion are very often strictures on religiosity, on superficial piety, on the lip-service and ceremonialism which comfort folk too much, and which indeed hide them from the Truth, as Cantwell Smith suggests. Nevertheless, as has been indicated in the previous paragraph, it is

67

not feasible to dispense with the rituals which express faith, and to this extent it is not possible to jettison religion, so long that is as one is worshipping God. Indeed as Cantwell Smith brings out very well in his historical section, on the evolution of the idea of religion, its original significance was very closely related to practice, and to cults in particular. Thus there is a good ground for looking historically upon the idea of religion as to do with the gods and their worship (one reason why Theravadin Buddhists are sometimes a bit unwilling to use the word 'religion' of their system of belief, for the cult of the gods, is to say the least secondary – for which reason Cantwell Smith may not have been entirely correct in equating the Buddhist distaste for the concept with other forms of distaste). Thus unless it is being proposed that there should be a radically religionless Christianity, it is necessary to interpret the Gospel–religion contrast as meaning essentially (but of course I here simplify) the contrast between following the Gospel and practising religiosity. Religion is religiosity for this purpose, then. What though is meant by talking of a radically religionless Christianity? By this I mean a ban on those activities and ideas which are religious: on prayer, worship, the sacraments, sacramental preaching, altars, communion tables, church buildings, blessings, halleluiahs, hymns, ministrations to the sick and dying, funeral services, sacred weddings, baptisms, anathemas, intercessions, masses, crucifixes, pulpits, chasubles, bands, clerical collars, prostrations, readings from the Bible, the Bible, the prayer-book, creeds, dogmas, descriptions of God, sacred narratives, Good Fridays, Christmases, saints' days, places of pilgrimages – and so on. *None* of these could be permitted in a genuinely religionless Christianity. But at the heart: no worship. Obviously some of the acts and things I have listed are fairly peripheral and could be cut out (Protestantism has cut out quite a lot of them, the Society of Friends many more), but what is to be thought about is the cutting-out of all of them without exception. This would erase religion, and in particular the Christian religion. Could one then speak any more about Christianity? Only in the sense that moral action and attitudes somehow express the heart of the Christian faith; and this, though a common sentiment, is a false one, for the ethics of Christianity have largely to do with the way in which centrally religious values are superimposed upon morality. Thus one

68

must conclude that it is necessary to reject any rigid interpretation of the notion of a religionless Christianity. Incidentally it may be worth noting that the religionlessness thesis partly grew out of a theory about the provenance of religious institutions and practices, as being human products and indeed involving human projections (thus Barth learns from Feuerbach). It would of course take us too far afield to investigate such a theory, but it is obviously a crucial one in the scientific study of religion and thus in the long run for Christian theology (since theology must take account of the reflexive effect upon religion of the study of religion – a point which is very clear in the manner in which the attempt at a scientific historical investigation of the New Testament has resulted in a wave of new theologies, from Baur to Bultmann and beyond). In brief, then, it does not seem open to the theist to destroy utterly the practice of religion, and in particular worship. This is another way of saying that the concepts of God and worship are indissolubly linked.

2.18. *Christianity and change.* The foregoing conclusion should not, however, be taken to mean that there is just no possibility of Christianity's jettisoning its cult. I would not wish to deny that there can be revolutions in religious traditions, so that it might happen that Christianity should concentrate on ethical and other aspects of the received faith rather than on worship and the sacraments. It might be odd to call the new non-religion Christianity, but if enough people did so, and traced their loyalty to Christ, then the revolution might have to be accepted, just as Marxism–Leninism becomes transformed into Maoism. But if such a revolution did happen, the old forms of words would subside into metaphor. 'God' would be a symbol of the good; the suffering servant would be the hero of a poem; the rituals would be dramas to remind the participants of the past, but sentimentally; the dog-collar would be simply the badge of one kind of organiser. I am not, then, denying this as a possibility; nor am I denying that people might intend this as a continuation of Christianity (so that intentionally in a certain sense it would be); but I am on the other hand affirming that a colossal conceptual revolution would in fact have been wrought. My analysis hitherto is predicated on the assumption that the religions have not yet met this revolution, and that we are still talking about God and worship in a more than metaphorical sense.

2.19. *The same God?* I now turn to the other main aspect of the thesis being offered by Cantwell Smith, which I shall crudely interpret as meaning that people of different faiths, such as the Christian, Muslim and Vaishnavite, in fact worship the same God. What are the criteria of sameness? Partly Cantwell Smith depends on a certain theory and it is quite an instructive one. Roughly it amounts to this: that the transcendent and historical processes dialectically interact, or, putting the matter rather more personally, an individual experiences or encounters the transcendent and responds with faith, this faith being expressed in ways derived from his cumulative tradition. He puts the matter as follows (p. 192):

> I certainly do not deny, then, that Christians in their religious life have something in common – or Muslims or any group, or indeed all men together. What rather I am asserting (conformably both to the historian, who cannot see that common element, and to the man of faith, who therein can) is that what they have in common lies not in the tradition that introduces them to transcendence, not in their faith by which they personally respond, but in that to which they respond, the transcendent itself.

2.20. *Disposing of the faith–observation dichotomy.* One aspect of Cantwell Smith's thinking here needs to be looked at briefly: he argues, as the passage indicates, that certain things are accessible to the faithful, but not to the outside observer – thus hell, he claims, is real to the faithful, but a merely human belief to the outsider, and so on. The distinction, however, seems to evaporate if one adopts sensitively the method of 'participant observation' or 'make-believe' such as anthropologists and historians of religion can use in revealing and evoking the phenomenological objects (the Foci) of rituals, etc. I shall then leave on one side this aspect of Cantwell Smith's thinking; it is not in any event very crucial to his main position, although it helps to make it unfalsifiable, alas.

2.21. *The transcendent and God.* Cantwell Smith speaks of a single transcendent to which human beings respond. Is this core identical with God? Can one argue that because various Foci of faith share a given property, namely transcendence, that they are identical? (There is a similar question about, say, Otto's account of the Holy: does it follow that because various Foci are numinous, they really are the same?) We need not here worry too much that the property in question is not clearly defined, and has an air of empty abstraction about it. We are more concerned with the logic of asserting that what different men worship really is the same Being. But what is necessary is to observe that the property or properties singled out as indicating that A and B are identical will be less ramified than those which are taken by adherents to describe A and B. That is, since each of the two Foci is delineated by an organic web of doctrine, myth and indeed practice, it has a rich and complex character, different from the rich and complex character of B. Thus the unitive core is, so to say, less than either of the full complexities. Thus the transcendent is not, in one sense, God. This implies that anyone who holds the identity-thesis predicated on a core needs to give some kind of explanation of how the non-core elements in A and B arose. It might be for instance that A is truly God, and that the non-core elements of B have arisen because of some mistake on the part of the adherents of B. Or it might be that both groups of adherents have imposed character-istics on the Foci (Focus) which are superfluous. It may be possible to treat the core as being something 'from the other side', the eternal, and the descriptions of the core given in ramified theologies as human constructs produced partly in response to encounters with the transcendent. It is a question to know how far any of these positions would be testable. The first would need to be backed by a theological criterion; it is in effect one theology's interpretation of another. The second would require us to isolate the core in suitable circumstances so that we could (so to say) have a look at the way the human reaction to it works itself out, with special reference to the way in which an existing cumulative tradition may be used to articulate the response. The difficulty is that with such a 'thin' account of the core, as the transcendent, it is impossible to separate out the core – it always comes overlaid with interpretations, drenched in them. Does it then become easier if we take some 'richer' mark of the core, for example the idea that God is creator of the universe? Thus since A is so described, and B, there is reason to suppose that A and B are identical.

2.22. *Remarks on religious identity.* Quite a notable feature of religions is their identifying one thing with another. Thus there

71

is the famous synthesis in the *Upaniṣads* which culminates in the identification of Brahman with the Atman. There is the identification of various gods within the Veda. There is the identification (in a sense, through the doctrine of *avatars*) of Krishna with Viṣṇu. There is the identification of all the Buddhas in the *dharmakāya* in Mahayana Buddhism. There is the identification of Christ and the Father in Christianity . . . and so on. I do not deny of course that the modes of identification differ somewhat (sometimes A is one with B and yet also in some respect not one with B, as is brought out in the Trinitarian formula – three entities in one substance). Now it is notable that these identities are not always predicated on very obvious resemblances. It is rather that there may be analogies; and there may also be arguments not directly depending on such likenesses. Thus for instance one of the reasons for the identification of all the Buddhas in the *dharmakāya* is that a Buddha in attaining enlightenment has a non-dual (*advaya*) experience of the Absolute (the Void, Suchness). in this 'emptiness' there are no distinctions, so that there is no distinction between the essence of one Buddha and another. But roughly one can say that such identities have religious grounds arising from within the dynamics of the systems in which they are found (but not all systems contain such identities). Also the identities allow, so to say, a reasonable tolerance as to what can be identified with what – they can, thus, surprise us (like the surprise that Jesus, a man, is also God). This relative looseness of fit, then, would not discourage us when it comes to trying to determine whether men in differing cultures worship the same God.

2.23. *Restrictions on identifications.* The upshot of the discussion so far is that one would need to consider the religious grounding of any proposed identity-claim as between the Foci of two cultures. But this should not prevent us from seeing that there will be elements of contradiction between two systems – not just beliefs that collide, but also practical injunctions. For the Christian it is not necessary to abstain from alcohol; for the Muslim it is. For the one, a pilgrimage to Mecca is not even encouraged; for the other it is, given the means, *de rigueur*. For one pacifism may have to be taken much more seriously than for the other. For one, one wife; for the other, maybe more. For one Christ is God; for the other this claim is blasphemous. What good is then achieved by saying that the two worship the same

God? If the concept of God is ramified organically, then it is not possible to say that God and Allah are the same (it might be argued). However, what is happening in any claimed identity is something more subtle: there is at work a process of abstraction – for instance singling out various key features of Allah and matching them to key features of God. The trouble is that the more systems you try to cover – the more 'universal' your ecumencity is – the more abstract the core becomes, until we have some such notion as the transcendent, as used by Cantwell Smith. On the hither side it becomes equally abstract: one has to talk about a 'response' to the transcendent. It is not even possible to use the general category of worship, for in Theravada Buddhism the main Focus, *nibbāna*, is not worshipped (it hardly makes sense to speak of this). Thus there are restrictions of two sorts upon the fruitfulness of making identifications. One is that full identification is not possible because of contradictions in the respective full ramified concepts (of God and of Allah, say); the other is that at the lower end – reaching a degree of abstraction in the description of the identified being leads to vacuity. It should, by the way, be noted that the upper restriction arises from contradictions (especially where these involve practical ones), not from mere *differences* between concepts. For identity statements when they are not tautologies or use proper names do exactly this – to apply two different concepts to the same entity.

2.24. *Religious grounds for identifications.* As was pointed out above, there are religious grounds for identifications. There is no exception to be made in the case of determining whether people of different traditions worship the same god. Thus ultimately the question becomes: from what point of view and for what reasons do we say that X and Y are the same God? Typically it is from the point of view of someone or some group in one religious tradition, attempting to give a theological interpretation of what goes on elsewhere. It is (true) possible that the claim could be made from a new religious position not specially tied to any of the traditions. If successful, such a claim helps to create an extra faith over and above those others which it interprets, so that one ends in a very like state of affairs. This being so, we can treat identity-claims as essentially theological, rather than phenomenological. This is not to deny of course that phenomenological descriptions, etc., are important; indeed they are if the theology that is being framed is to look realistic in terms of the facts of human belief and practice.

2.25. *Some concluding remarks.* Our investigation of the nature of worship and its objects is intended to exhibit the close conceptual connection between gods or God on the one hand and the practice of worship on the other. It is from this point of view that we have been critical of attempts to present analyses of religious faith and language which fail to stress the ritual process. This is to wrench the concept of God from its living milieu. I am not denying that a religion might change and subtly change its concept of God – alter it ultimately beyond recognition if a 'religionless' solution were accepted. The history of religions acquaints us with cases of such radical alteration, and though the later phase may appeal to the earlier this does not disguise the change in substance (consider the Magi and later Zoroastrianism in relation to early Zoroastrianism; consider the Buddha and Nichiren). But what I am claiming is that the substantive concept of God is indissolubly linked to the practice of worship. Yet is this apparent in much of recent philosophy of religion in the analytic mode? It is not clear in Hare's blik analysis; it is not clear in 'Gods' by Wisdom; it is not clear in Ramsey's account of penny-dropping experiences; it is opaque in Flew's *God and Philosophy*, and not much evident in C. B. Martin's *Religious Belief*. Though these works have very clear merits in their differing ways, they have yet failed to place religious belief in what I have called its living milieu. Perhaps the worship and the sacraments have been taken for granted. But I would think it unwise to neglect them, for religion's purchase on the world lies in practice and practice has to do with these things. However important moral action may be, and political action in these dark latter days, one cannot reduce Christianity or any other religion to such action. One cannot 'do a Braithwaite' on them. For the net result of doing this is to rob religion of its cutting-edge; it collapses into a kind of humanist ethic – a very fine thing, of course, but not to be confused with Christianity (etc.).

2.26. *Does God then depend on us?* If God is conceptually related in the way I have described to ritual, then cessation of ritual might be thought to destroy God. Is God dependent on us, just as colours are mind-dependent? Of course it would be absurd to suppose that God ceases when our prayers do; this would in any case be inconsistent with the spirit of what is said in the prayers themselves. But God is reached down a certain corridor, according to my analysis, and this is the corridor of worship (just as *nirvana* is reached along the corridor of contemplation). The question, however, as to whether God depends on us is tied heavily with the whole question of the truth of religious statements. This is too large a topic for me to have dealt with here. I have tried a much humbler task: to show some of the factors which have to be taken into account in understanding religious concepts and so in trying to determine the criteria of truth in religion. One must understand before one can determine on what basis one should believe, or disbelieve. *Intelligo ut . . . ?*

References

(Numbers refers to the paragraphs)

1.2 N. Smart, *Reasons and Faiths* (Routledge & Kegan Paul, London, 1958).

1.6 N. Smart, 'Gods, Bliss and Morality', in I. T. Ramsey (ed), *Christian Ethics and Contemporary Philosophy* (S.C.M. Press, London, 1966).

1.7 Mary Douglas, *Purity and Danger* (Penguin Books, Harmondsworth, 1970).

1.12 M. Yinger, *The Scientific Study of Religion* (Collier–Macmillan, London, 1970).

1.18 N. Smart, 'Myth and Transcendence', *Monist*, I, 4 (1966).

1.32 N. Smart, *The Yogi and the Devotee* (Allen & Unwin, London, 1968).

1.33 R. Otto, *The Idea of the Holy*, 2nd ed. (Oxford U.P., 1950).

1.36 D. Evans, *The Logic of Self-Involvement* (S.C.M. Press, London, 1963).

1.37 Smart, *Reasons and Faiths*.

1.63 D. Z. Phillips, *The Concept of Prayer* (Routledge & Kegan Paul, London, 1965).

2.1 J. N. Findlay, 'Can God's Existence be Disproved?', *Mind*, n.s., LVII (1948) 179, reprinted in A. G. N. Flew and A. MacIntyre (eds), *New Essays in Philosophical Theology* (S.C.M. Press, London, 1955).

2.5 C. B. Martin, *Religious Belief* (Cornell U.P., Ithaca, N.Y., 1959), and 'The Perfect Good', in Flew and MacIntyre (eds), *New Essays in Philosophical Theology*.

2.8 N. Malcolm, 'Anselm's Ontological Arguments', *Philosophical Review*, LXIX 1 (1960) 41–62.

2.10 S. Kierkegaard, *The Journals*, ed. A. Dru (Oxford U.P., 1938) s. 936.

2.14 W. Cantwell Smith, *The Meaning and End of Religion*, new ed. (New English Library, London, 1966).

2.15 N. Smart, *Doctrine and Argument in Indian Philosophy* (Allen & Unwin, London, 1964).

2.17 H. Kraemer, *The Christian Message in a Non-Christian World* (Edinburgh House Press, London, 1938).

2.25 A. G. N. Flew, *God and Philosophy* (Hutchinson, London, 1966).